THE FRACTAL STRUCTURE OF DATA REFERENCE
OF DATA REFERENCE
Applications to the Memory Hierarchy

The Kluwer International Series on
ADVANCES IN DATABASE SYSTEMS

Series Editor
Ahmed K. Elmagarmid

Purdue University
West Lafayette, IN 47907

Other books in the Series:

THE FRACTAL STRUCTURE OF DATA REFERENCE
Applications to the Memory Hierarchy

by

Bruce McNutt
International Business Machines Corporation
San Jose, California, U.S.A.

KLUWER ACADEMIC PUBLISHERS
Boston / Dordrecht / London

Distributors for North, Central and South America:
Kluwer Academic Publishers
101 Philip Drive
Assinippi Park
Norwell, Massachusetts 02061 USA
Telephone (781) 871-6600   Fax (781) 681-9045
E-Mail <kluwer@wkap.com>

Distributors for all other countries:
Kluwer Academic Publishers Group
Distribution Centre
Post Office Box 322
3300 AH Dordrecht, THE NETHERLANDS
Telephone 31 78 6392 392   Fax 31 78 6392 254
E-Mail <services@wkap.nl>

   Electronic Services <http://www.wkap.nl>

The following are trademarks or registered trademarks of IBM Corporation:
IBM, CICS, DB2, Hiperspace, IMS, OS/390, VM/ESA.
Tivoli is a registered trademark Tivoli Systems, Inc.
CA-ASTEX is a registered trademark of Computer Associates, Inc.
SAS is a registered trademark of SAS Institute, Inc.
Windows NT is a registered trademark of Microsoft Corporation.

Library of Congress Cataloging-in-Publication Data

McNutt, Bruce, 1951-
   The fractal structure of data reference : applications to the memory hierarchy / Bruce McNutt.
      p. cm. -- (The Kluwer international series on advances in database systems ; 22)
   Includes bibliographical references and index.

   1. Database management . 2. Data structures (Computer science) 3. Memory hierarchy
(Computer science) I. Title. II. Series.

QA76.9.D3 M398 2000   ISBN 978-1-4419-4998-1
005.74–dc   e-ISBN 978-0-306-47034-9   00-057836

Printed on acid-free paper.

Printed in the United States of America

*The Publisher offers discounts on this book for course use and bulk purchases. For
further information, send email to <scott.delman@wkap.com>.*

This book is dedicated to the system programmers who, as survey participants, donated their time and skills to advance everyone's understanding of disk workloads.

Contents

List of Figures

List of Tables

Preface

For purposes of understanding its performance, a computer system is traditionally viewed as a processor coupled to one or more disk storage devices, and driven by externally generated requests (typically called *transactions*). Over the past several decades, very powerful techniques have become available to the performance analyst attempting to understand, at a high level, the operational behavior of such systems.

Nevertheless, the ability of computers to rapidly deliver requested information, at the time it is needed, depends critically on an underlying structure whose operational behavior is not nearly as well understood: the *memory hierarchy* through which data stored on disk is made available to the processor. The memory hierarchy tends to consist of many levels, including one or more processor buffer memories (also called L1 and L2 cache), main processor memory, disk storage cache memory, disk storage, and often tape. A given level is usually configured to have both a much smaller storage capacity and a much faster access time than the level below it. The data stored in each memory level is managed dynamically, with new data being brought in as needed from the level below.

The architectural concept of a memory hierarchy has been immensely successful, making possible today's spectacular pace of technology evolution in both the volume of data *and* the average speed of data access. As we shall find in Chapter 1, however, its success is difficult to understand if we rely upon a traditional performance modeling framework. This is because the power of a memory hierarchy comes from its ability to take advantage of patterns of data use that are *transient*. Repeated requests tend to be made to a given data item over a short period of time, after which the data may remain unreferenced for extended periods (or even indefinitely). Such patterns do not yield easily to an analysis based upon steady-state, "memoryless" behavior.

This book adopts a *heavy-tailed* distribution for the time between requests to a given data item: substantial probabilities are assigned even to very long interarrival times. The probabilities are sufficiently high, and the corresponding gaps between arrivals are sufficiently long, that the average time until the next reference becomes unbounded. There is *no* steady-state arrival rate. This modeling approach reflects the opposite of the usual steady-state assumptions: arrivals are attributed to transient events, rather than to an ongoing arrival process.

In a reflection of its emphasis on transient events, the proposed modeling approach calls for a very high arrival probability during the time shortly after a request. The probability then falls off rapidly, if no request occurs. This results in a pattern of accesses characterized by short "bursts", separated by long periods of inactivity. By studying such transient "bursts", we are able to gain a practical understanding of memory hierarchy performance.

Heavy-tailed distributions are characteristic of fractal, or self-similar, phenomena. As discussed in Chapter 1, the presence of self-similarity in data reference patterns should not be surprising; indeed, it would be reasonable to anticipate it based upon the explicitly hierarchical nature of most software. To reflect the inferred "behind the scenes" role of hierarchically structured software, we adopt, in Chapter 1, the term *hierarchical reuse model* to describe the overall modeling framework which this book proposes. We also show that the proposed heavy-tailed distribution provides an excellent approximation of realistic interarrival times to individual data items.

Even without the arguments of Chapter 1, self-similar behavior would *still* be plausible, or even likely. Such behavior has now been observed in *many* aspects of data reference [1, 2, 3, 4, 5, 6, 7]. The pioneering work by Voldman, Mandelbrot, and others [1], and later by Thiébaut [2], is particularly worth noting, since it established that the sequence of locations referenced by software tends to be structured in a self-similar manner. This fact certainly enhances the plausibility of a self-similar relationship involving interarrival times to any single, identified reference location.

Despite the importance of self-similar phenomena in describing the operational behavior of computer systems, however, this preface is perhaps the place to admit that the demonstration of one more example of such a phenomenon is not, by itself, sufficiently interesting to justify an entire book. Instead, the "meat" of the present book comes from the ability of the hierarchical reuse model to impose a mathematically tractable structure on important problems involving the operation and performance of a memory hierarchy. We shall obtain striking insights into how such hierarchies work, and how to exploit them to best advantage. The emphasis of the book will be on the practical applications of such results.

The focus of the applications examined in this book is on the portion of a computer system's memory hierarchy that lies below the level of the "get" and "put" statements issued by running software. This includes file buffer areas in main processor memory, cache memory associated with the disk system, disk storage, and tape when it is used as a repository for dynamic migration and recall.

The primary audience intended for the book is the large body of workers who endeavor to ensure that computer systems, and the associated disk storage, are configured and managed so as to deliver the expected and desired level of performance. This includes practitioners in the area of computer performance management and capacity planning, as well as those who build tools to facilitate their work.

To apply many of the ideas presented in this book, performance practitioners will require some minimal level of storage subsystem performance reporting (for example, measurements of cache hit ratios). On subsystems running under the Operating System/390 (OS/390) and Virtual Machine (VM) operating systems, the needed reporting is universal and standardized. For this reason, these environments are the main source of the case studies, empirical data, and examples presented in the book. Performance practitioners working on the Unix and Windows NT platforms will also find, in many cases, that the needed performance reporting can be obtained. Although it is not standardized across storage vendors, vendors often offer such reporting as a differentiating feature.

As befits a work about fractal modeling, the chapters of the book cover events that play out at a wide range of time scales. The first five chapters focus on the operation of file buffers and disk cache; memory residency times at this time scale range from a few seconds to several minutes. Among these five chapters, those seeking a quick introduction to the most important ideas should select Chapter 1 (fundamental modeling concepts), Chapter 3 (capacity planning for cache memory), and perhaps Chapter 2 (a concrete illustration of hierarchical reuse behavior). Chapters 4 (interaction of processor file buffers and storage control cache) and 5 (cache memory management) cover additional topics important to performance specialists.

We then gradually lengthen the time scale. Chapter 6 considers the collection of free space in a log-structured disk array; here the time scales range from minutes to days. Chapters 7 and 8 examine the life cycle of disk storage files, and their management via migration and recall; this involves time scales ranging from hours to months. Chapter 7 also explores the limits of the hierarchical reuse model, by identifying patterns of data item use which appear to be more persistent than the hierarchical reuse model would suggest.

Finally, Chapter 9 develops a fresh way to look at the planning for disk storage, based upon viewing entire *applications* from a statistical standpoint (as though they were objects belonging at some deep level within a memory hierarchy, operating on a time scale of months to years). This allows important insights to be gained about how to strike an overall balance between disk storage capacity, cost, and performance.

BRUCE MCNUTT

Acknowledgments

The author would like to acknowledge the vital roles played by Mr. Jeffrey Berger, Mrs. Neena A. Cherian, Mr. Joe Hyde, and Mr. Charlie Werner, each of whom developed key tracing or trace analysis software without which the investigations reported in the present book would not have been possible.

In many stimulating discussions, at the annual conference of the Computer Measurement Group and elsewhere, individuals have shared their views and comments on the topics presented in the book. This input was invaluable in organizing the presentation of ideas. The author would like to thank all of those who did so, including especially Dr. H. Pat Artis, Dr. Alexandre Brandwajn, Mr. Mark Friedman, Dr. Gilbert Houtekamer, Mr. David L. Peterson, and Mr. Brian J. Smith. Thanks also to Mr. David A. Short and again to Brian Smith for their help with editing the manuscript.

Chapter 1

HIERARCHICAL REUSE MODEL

The ability of computers to rapidly deliver requested information, at the time it is needed, depends critically on the *memory hierarchy* through which data stored on disk is made available to the processor. The organization of storage into a hierarchy has made possible today's spectacular pace of technology evolution in both the volume of data *and* the average speed of data access. But the effectiveness of a memory hierarchy depends, in turn, upon the patterns of data reference that it must support. The purpose of this chapter is to develop a practical description of data reference patterns, suitable for use in analyzing the performance of a memory hierarchy.

After filling in some essential background and terminology, we shall first show that the traditional "memoryless" model of interarrivals does *not* offer the practical description we are looking for. Indeed, this approach is not even able to predict something as fundamental as the advantages offered by organizing memory into a hierarchy — which every computer architect today takes for granted on the basis of practical experience.

As an alternative, we develop the *hierarchical reuse model*. This description of data reference uses a heavy-tailed distribution of interarrival times, to reflect *transient* patterns of access. We show that such an approach both makes sense, and fits well with empirical data. Its power as a tool for analysis becomes apparent as we study the cache visits made by data stored on disk, and the resulting requirements for cache memory.

Finally, we extend our analysis to a memory hierarchy containing three or more levels, with emphasis on the important special case in which disk storage requests are buffered using both host file buffers as well as storage control cache.

1.   BACKGROUND

Although the concepts discussed in the present chapter apply broadly to memory and storage hierarchies within many computing platforms, we shall draw our examples and empirical data from the caching of disk storage references running under the VM and OS/390 operating systems. In these environments, communication with disk storage conforms to the *Extended Count-Key-Data* (ECKD) protocol.

For the purpose of access via this protocol, individual application records are grouped logically into *track images*. Originally, track images were mapped 1-to-1 with physical disk tracks, but this is no longer the case with current disk storage subsystems. Most commonly, for production database applications, one track image contains twelve records, each 4096 bytes (one *page*) in size. When a request occurs for data located in a given track image (or more loosely, when a request occurs to a given track), a cached storage subsystem first attempts to find the track in cache memory. If this lookup is successful (a cache *hit*), then the subsystem can respond to the request immediately, with no delays for physical disk access. If the lookup is unsuccessful (a cache *miss*), then the subsystem *stages* the track image from physical disk into memory. The central measures of cache effectiveness are the *miss ratio* (fraction of I/O's that require staging) and its complement, the *hit ratio* (fraction of I/O's that can be serviced directly from cache).

For the purpose of analyzing memory hierarchy behavior, we shall assume a "plain vanilla" cache for storing track images. By "plain vanilla", we mean that the entire track is staged when it is found to be absent from cache; that such staging occurs for both read as well as write misses; and that cache memory is managed by applying the *Least Recently Used* (LRU) replacement criterion, as described in the immediately following paragraph, to identify the next track to displace from memory when performing a stage. These assumptions accurately describe many models of cached storage controls. Also, we shall find that it is not difficult to refine them, when necessary, to better model the operation of a specific controller, as long as the key assumption of LRU management is retained.

The LRU scheme for managing cache memory is virtually universal for disk storage cache. This scheme imposes a linked list structure, called the *LRU list*, onto the stored track images. The linked list is represented via pointers, so that tracks can change their logical list positions without moving physically. When a cache miss causes a new track to enter the cache, it is placed (logically) at one end of the linked list, called the *top*, or *Most Recently Used* (MRU) position. When a cache hit occurs, the requested track it is moved from its current list position to the top (except in the case that the track is already at the top, making this operation unnecessary). After either a hit or a miss, tracks in the middle of the LRU list, other than the requested track, remain linked together in the same order as before.

This algorithm has the net effect that the tracks in the list always appear in order of the time since the last reference to them — the track at the MRU position was used most recently, the track next on the list was used most recently before the MRU track, and so forth. The track at the opposite end of the list, called the *bottom*, or *Least Recently Used* (LRU) position, is the track for which the longest time has passed since the previous reference. Therefore, in the LRU algorithm, the track at the bottom position is the one displaced when memory must be freed to bring a new track into the cache.

2. MOTIVATION

Suppose, now, that we put ourselves into the shoes of a storage architect of many years ago, trying to assess whether cache memory of the type just described is a worth-while investment of time and effort, and whether the resulting increment in product cost can be justified. As a basis for the analysis, let us adopt the *independent reference model* to describe the pattern of track references. This model was first introduced by Coffman and Denning [8], and is still in active use for cache analysis [9].

The architects responsible for introducing the early models of disk storage cache relied primarily on trace-based simulations to develop an understanding of cache operation. Nevertheless, let us consider what conclusions might have been drawn from the independent reference model, if it had been applied to an analysis of the proposed cache technology.

The objective of the proposed cache design, which we now wish to evaluate, is to speed up the average disk service time by using a small quantity of semiconductor memory whose access speed is much faster than that of the underlying disk storage. More specifically, using numbers characteristic of the original storage control cache memories introduced in the early 1980's, let us assume that we can provide 16 megabytes of cache on a disk storage subsystem of 20 gigabytes. Thus, we can deliver a ratio of semiconductor memory, relative to disk storage, equal to .0008. To be effective in boosting performance, we also require that at least 70 percent of the requests must be hits [11]. (More recent cache memories are larger and can function effectively with lower hit ratios, but the numbers just stated, although out of date, provide an interesting real-life case study).

To evaluate the proposed design, we shall apply the *independent reference model*. This "memoryless" model states that every I/O reference represents an independent, identically distributed multinomial random variable, whose outcome is the location of the next referenced track. Thus, arrivals to any given track must occur at a specific average rate, which is directly proportional to the probability of requesting the track (more specifically, the arrival rate of requests to a given track equals its probability of being referenced times the overall rate of requests).

Given these assumptions, there is a simple upper bound on the percentage of hits that can be achieved in the cache. To obtain this bound, sort the tracks in descending order by the rate of track references. Let N be the total number of tracks, and consider the subset $first_L$ of tracks, given by the first $L < N$ that appear on the sorted list. Then clearly, by the independence of references, no subset of L tracks other than $first_L$ can have a higher probability of containing the next request.

Setting $l = L/N$, let us define $\Omega(l)$ to be the fraction of the total request rate attributable to $first_L$. Thus, the statement $\Omega(.1) = .5$ would mean that fifty percent of the total requests are to data contained in the busiest ten percent of the tracks. Since the beginning of the sorted list represents the best possible cache contents, we may apply the definition of $\Omega(l)$ to obtain the following upper bound on the hit ratio h:

$$h \leq \Omega(l_c) \tag{1.1}$$

where $l_c \approx .0008$ is the fraction of disk tracks capable of being stored in cache.

By (1.1), we are now forced to conclude that *in order for the proposed cache to function effectively, at least seventy percent of the references must go to no more than .08 percent of the tracks.*

In view of the diversity of system usage that occurs from moment to moment in a production computing environment, this picture of a permanent, *very* narrowly focused pattern of access would seem to be in conflict with common sense. Nevertheless, early caches of the type just outlined *did* function effectively in many environments (although, for some environments, they were too small). In those environments where the early cache designs were successful, does it follow, despite the apparent conflict with common sense, that most activity was indeed concentrated in such a small percentage of tracks?

If so, then our next conclusion must be that, even after all of the time and effort invested in its design, a memory hierarchy was unnecessary. Rather than build a dynamically managed hierarchy, we could have accomplished the same results more easily by dedicating each memory resource to contain specific, identified types of data.

A real-life comparison between these two alternative strategies is provided by the history of disk storage products during the 1980's and early 1990's. Two contrasting schemes for deploying semiconductor memory in a disk storage environment were offered in the marketplace. One design, as just outlined, was based upon the concept of a memory hierarchy. The other, based upon dedicated memory resources, offered stand-alone products which could emulate disk storage using semiconductor memory. Such products, usually called *solid state disks* (SSD's), were intended for use as one part of a larger storage configuration. They provided storage for those data deemed to require maximum performance.

In the market of the late 1990's, cached storage controls have become very widely accepted, while few SSD's remain in use. Indeed, one important storage vendor owes its present success to a strategic shift of its product line to a cached, rather than dedicated-memory, design.

In [10], Henley compares directly the gains in performance that can be achieved with a memory hierarchy to those which can be achieved with equivalent amounts of disk and semiconductor storage managed separately. In a realistic computing environment, Henley found from analysis of traces that the effectiveness of a given amount of semiconductor memory is *many times* greater when it is incorporated into a memory hierarchy, compared to its effectiveness when allocated in static fashion. This is due to the ability of a memory hierarchy to dynamically adapt to short-term patterns of use.

The disparity in effectiveness between the memory-hierarchy and dedicated-use strategies shows that our previous conclusion (1.1) is badly flawed. To make further progress in understanding the operation of a memory hierarchy, we must first find some alternative to the independent reference model upon which (1.1) is based.

The *hierarchical reuse model*, which we shall propose in the following section, defines a distribution of track interarrival times with a tail so heavy that the mean interarrival time becomes unbounded. As a result, all activity is treated as being transient in nature. A given track has *no* steady-state arrival rate. The function $\Omega(l)$, in terms of which (1.1) is stated, can no longer be defined.

In another sharp contrast to the independent reference model, the hierarchical reuse model is far from memoryless. The probability of requesting a given data item is *not* fixed with time. Instead, it depends strongly upon the amount of time that has passed since the previous reference.

In a study of any large collection of data items (such as all of the tracks in a storage subsystem), over some defined period of time, references to many or most of them will, in general, have occurred prior to the beginning of the period. We shall take the times of such references to be unknown. This means that the aggregate arrival rate for the system as a whole will not be obtainable from the interarrival distribution, and must be measured or specified separately.

This "disconnect" between arrival rate and interarrival characteristics, which many workers in the field of performance modeling may initially find strange, is in fact exactly what is needed to allow the modeling of transient patterns of access. It is the price that we choose to pay to correct the severe and fundamental modeling errors which would otherwise flow from (1.1).

3.   MODEL DEFINITION

Eventually, this book will present abundant statistical summaries of data reference patterns. As a starting point, however, let us begin with a single, observed pattern of access to a single item of data. Figure 1.1 presents one such pattern, among hundreds of thousands, observed in a large, production database environment running under OS/390. In Figure 1.1, the horizontal axis is a time line, upon which most of the requests are marked. When a group of requests are too closely spaced to distinguish along the time line, the second and subsequent requests are displaced vertically to give a "zoom" of each one's interarrival time with respect to the request before it.

A careful examination of Figure 1.1 makes it clear that the arrivals are driven by processes operating at several distinct time scales. For example, episodes occur repeatedly in which the interarrival time is a matter of a few milliseconds; such "bursts" are separated, in turn, by interarrival times of many seconds or tens of seconds. Finally, the entire sequence is widely separated from any other reference to the data.

If we now examine the structure of database software, in an effort to account for data reuse at a variety of time scales, we find that we need not look far. For example, data reuse may occur due to repeated requests in the same subroutine, different routines called to process the same transaction, or multiple transactions needed to carry out some overall task at the user level. The explicitly hierarchical structure of most software provides a simple and compelling ex-

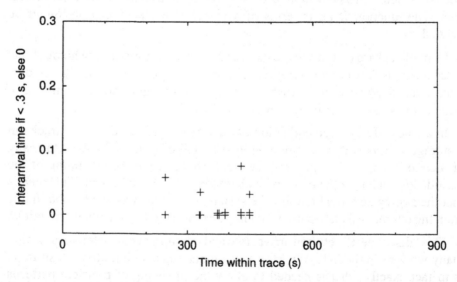

Figure 1.1. Pattern of requests to an individual track. The vertical axis acts as a "zoom", to separate groups of references that are too closely spaced to distinguish along a single time line.

planation for the apparent presence of multiple time scales in reference patterns such as the one presented by Figure 1.1.

Although the pattern of events might well differ between one time scale and the next, it seems reasonable to explore the simplest model, in which the various time scales are *self-similar*. Let us therefore adopt the view that the pattern of data reuse at long time scales should mirror that at short time scales, once the time scale itself is taken into account.

To explore how to apply this idea, consider two tracks:

1. a *short-term* track, last referenced 5 seconds ago.

2. a *long-term* track, last referenced 20 seconds ago.

Based upon the idea of time scales that are mirror images of each other, we should expect that the short term track has the same probability of being referenced in the next 5 seconds, as the long term track does of being referenced in the next 20 seconds. Similarly, we should expect that the short term track has the same probability of being referenced in the next 1 minute, as the long-term track does of being referenced in the next 4 minutes.

By formalizing the above example, we are now ready to state a specific hypothesis. Let the random variable U be the time from the last use of a given track to the next reuse. Then we define the *hierarchical reuse* model of arrivals to the track as the hypothesis that the conditional distribution of the quantity

$$\frac{U}{\delta_0} | U > \delta_0 \tag{1.2}$$

does not depend upon δ_0. Moreover, we shall also assume, for simplicity, that this distribution is independent and identical across periods following different references.

Clearly, a hypothesis of this form must be constructed with some lower limit on the time scale δ_0; otherwise, we are in danger of dividing by zero. A lower limit of this kind ends up applying to most self-similar models of real phenomena [12]. For the applications pursued in this book, the lower limit appears to be much less than any of the time scales of interest (some fraction of one second). Thus, we will not bother trying to quantify the lower limit but simply note that there is one. In the remainder of the book, we shall avoid continually repeating the caveat that a lower limit exists to the applicable time scale; instead, the reader should take it for granted that this caveat applies.

By good fortune, the type of statistical self-similarity that is based upon an invariant distribution of the form (1.2) is well understood. Indeed, Mandelbrot has shown that a random variable U which satisfies the conditions stated in the hierarchical reuse hypothesis must belong to the *heavy-tailed*, also called *hyperbolic*, family of distributions. This means that the asymptotic behavior of U must tend toward that of a power law:

$$P[U > \delta] = a\delta^{-\theta} \tag{1.3}$$

where $a > 0$ and $\theta > 0$ are constants that depend upon the specific random variable being examined. Distributions having this form, first studied by Italian economist/sociologist Vilfredo Pareto (1848-1923) and French mathematician Paul Lévy (1886-1971), differ sharply from the more traditional probability distributions such as exponential and normal. Non-negligible probabilities are assigned even to extreme outcomes. In a distribution of the form (1.3), it is possible for both the variance (if $\theta \leq 2$) and the mean (if $\theta \leq 1$) to become unbounded.

As just discussed in the previous section, our objective is to reflect a transient pattern of access, characterized by the absence of steady-state arrivals. For this reason, our interest is focused specifically on the range of parameter values $\theta \leq 1$ for which the distribution of interarrival times, as given by (1.3), lacks a finite mean. For mathematical convenience, we also choose to exclude the case $\theta = 1$, in which the mean interarrival time "just barely" diverges. Thus, in this book we shall be interested in the behavior of (1.3) in the range $0 < \theta < 1$.

The first thing to observe about (1.3), in the context of a memory hierarchy, is that it is actually two statements in one. To make this clear, imagine a storage control cache operating under a steady load, and consider the time spent in the cache by a track that is referenced exactly once. Such a track gradually progresses from the top to the bottom of the LRU list, and is finally displaced by a new track being staged in. Given that the total time for this journey through the LRU list is long enough to smooth out statistical fluctuations, this time should, to a reasonable approximation, always be the same.

Assume, for simplicity, that the time for a track to get from the top to the bottom of the LRU list, after exactly one reference has been made to it, is a constant. We shall call this quantity the *single-reference residency time*, or τ (recalling the earlier discussion about time scales, $\tau \geq \tau_{min} > 0$, where τ_{min} is some fraction of one second). It then follows that a request to a given track can be serviced out of cache memory if and only if the time since the previous reference to the track is no longer than τ. By applying this *criterion of time-in-cache* to distinguish hits and misses, any statement about the distribution of interarrival times must also be a statement about miss ratios. In particular, (1.3) is mirrored by the corresponding result:

$$m(\tau) = a\tau^{-\theta} \tag{1.4}$$

Actually, we can conclude even more than this, by considering how subsets of the stored data must share the use of the cache. The situation is analogous to that of a crowded road from one town to another, with one lane for each direction of traffic. Just as it must take all types of cars about the same amount of time to complete the journey between towns, it must take tracks containing all types of data about the same amount of time to get from the top to the bottom of the LRU list. Thus, if we wish to apply the hierarchical reuse model to some identified application specifically (say, application i), we may write

$$m_i(\tau) = a_i \tau^{-\theta_i} \tag{1.5}$$

where $m_i(\tau)$, a_i, and θ_i refer to the specific application, but where τ continues to represent the *global* single reference residency time of the cache as a whole.

The conclusion that τ determines the effectiveness of the cache, not just overall but for each individual application, is a result of the criterion of time-in-cache, and applies regardless of the exact distribution of interarrival times. Thus, a reasonable starting point in designing a cached storage configuration is to specify a minimum value for τ. This ensures that each application is provided with some defined, minimal level of service.

In Chapter 3, we shall also find that it works to specify a minimum value for the *average* time spent by a track in the cache (where the average includes both tracks referenced exactly once as well as tracks that are referenced more than once). The average residency time provides an attractive foundation for day-to-day capacity planning, for reasons that we will continue to develop in the present chapter, as well as in Chapter 3.

3.1   COMPARISON WITH EMPIRICAL DATA

Figure 1.2 presents a test of (1.3) against live data obtained during a survey of eleven moderate to large production VM installations [13].

When software running under the VM operating system makes an I/O request, the system intercepts the request and passes it to disk storage. This scheme reflects VM's design philosophy, in which VM is intended to provide a layer of services upon which other operating systems can run as *guests*. With the exception of an optional VM facility called minidisk cache, not used in the environments presented by Figure 1.2, a VM host system does not retain the results of previous I/O requests for potential use in servicing future I/O. This makes data collected on VM systems (other than those which use minidisk cache) particularly useful as a test of (1.3), since there is no processor cache to complicate the interpretation of the results. The more complex results obtained in OS/390 environments, where large file buffer areas have been set aside in processor memory, are considered in Subsection 5.1.

Figure 1.2 presents the distribution of interarrival times for the user and system data pools at each surveyed installation. Note that the plot is presented in log-log format (and also that the "up" direction corresponds to improving miss ratio values). If (1.3) were exact rather than approximate, then this presentation of the data should result in a variety of straight lines; the slope of each line (in the chart's "up" direction) would be the value of θ for the corresponding data pool.

Figure 1.2 comes strikingly close to being the predicted collection of straight lines. Thus, (1.3) provides a highly serviceable approximation. With rare exceptions, the slopes in the figure divide into two rough groups:

1. Slopes between 0.2 and 0.3. This group contains mainly application data, but also a few of the curves for system data.

2. Slopes between 0.3 and 0.4. This group consists almost entirely of system data

Suppose, now, that we want to estimate cache performance in a VM environment, and that data of the kind presented by Figure 1.2 are not available. In this case, we would certainly be pushing our luck to assume that the slopes in group (2) apply. Projected miss ratios based on this assumption would almost always be too optimistic, except for caches containing exclusively system data — and even for system data the projections might still be too optimistic! Thus, in the absence of further information it would be appropriate to assume a slope in the range of group (1). This suggests that the guestimate

$$\theta \approx 0.25 \tag{1.6}$$

is reasonable for rough planning purposes.

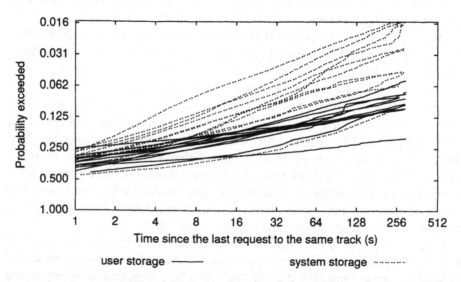

Figure 1.2.   Distribution of track interarrival times. Each curve shows a user or system storage pool at one of 11 surveyed VM installations.

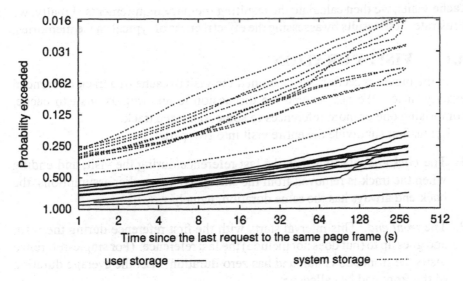

Figure 1.3. Distribution of page frame interarrival times. Each curve shows a user or system storage pool at one of 11 surveyed VM installations.

Figure 1.2 assumes that we are interested in a cache management scheme based upon track images. While a scheme of this type usually applies to storage control cache, however, the caching performed in host processor memory is normally based on smaller units of granularity. For example, the minidisk cache facility mentioned earlier manages data in units of one *page frame* (one block of 4096 bytes).

The unit of granularity used in managing the cache has an important effect upon its interarrival times and miss ratio. To illustrate the impact of cache granularity, Figure 1.3 presents the interarrival times observed at the page level of granularity, based upon the same traces as those presented in Figure 1.2. Note that at the page level of granularity, a reasonable guess for the value of θ would be roughly half of that obtained assuming cache management based upon tracks (thus, $\theta_{page} \approx 0.125$).

4.   VISITS TO MEMORY

So far, we have observed that data item interarrivals tend to exhibit a fractal structure. The present section shows that this fact, beyond being interesting in itself, is extremely helpful to the performance analyst. The power of (1.3) to solve practical problems comes from the simple and mathematically tractable statements that it yields about the time spent in memory during a cache visit.

We shall examine closely the structure of such visits, which the hierarchical reuse model predicts to be predominately transient. Based upon our analysis of cache visits, we then calculate the resulting memory requirements. Finally, we illustrate these results by assessing the effectiveness of typical cache memories.

4.1   VISIT DURATION

In the previous section, we examined the visit to cache of a track referenced exactly once. We now extend the discussion to an arbitrary visit to cache, comprising one or more references to some identified track.

Let us first subdivide the entire visit into two parts:

1. The *back end*, starting with the last reference during the visit, and ending when the track is removed from the cache. By our earlier assumptions, the back end always has the same duration, namely τ.

2. The *front end*. This interval starts with the first reference during the visit, and goes up to (but does not include) the last reference. (For single-reference visits the front end is null and has zero duration). Let the average duration of the front end be called $\Delta\tau$.

Thus, the total average duration of the visit as a whole is given by

$$T = \tau + \Delta\tau \tag{1.7}$$

Suppose, now, that the cumulative distribution function of the time U between references to a given track is $F(\cdot)$. We do not necessarily assume that F is given by (1.3); any distribution will do at this stage. Let

$$g(\tau) = \frac{1}{F(\tau)} \int_0^\tau x \, dF(x) \tag{1.8}$$

be the average length of time prior to a *hit* since the previous reference to the same track.

By definition, $\Delta\tau$ specifies the amount of front end time that passes per cache miss. Similarly, $g(\tau)$ specifies the amount of front end time that passes per cache hit. Letting r be the total rate of I/O requests, this gives two ways of calculating the total rate at which front end time occurs:

$$\Delta\tau \, rm(\tau) = g(\tau)r(1 - m(\tau))$$

or,

$$\Delta\tau = \frac{1 - m(\tau)}{m(\tau)} g(\tau) \tag{1.9}$$

This is a general result; it does not depend upon the assumption of hierarchical reuse probability.

If, however, we apply the hierarchical reuse model, we can calculate $g(\tau)$ by plugging

$$F(\tau) = 1 - m(\tau)$$
$$= 1 - a\tau^{-\theta} \qquad (1.10)$$

into (1.8). Due to the factor of x that appears in the integral, we choose a strategy of formal evaluation throughout its entire range, including values x approaching zero (which, although problematic from the standpoint of the model, are insignificant). This evaluation yields

$$g(\tau) = \frac{1}{1 - m(\tau)} \frac{\theta}{1 - \theta} a\tau^{1-\theta}$$

Substituting into (1.9) now gives

$$\Delta\tau = \tau \frac{\theta}{1 - \theta} \qquad (1.11)$$

Combining this result with (1.7), we therefore obtain

$$T = \frac{\tau}{1 - \theta} \qquad (1.12)$$

The average residency time is directly proportional to the single-reference residency time.

It is important to note that, for typical values of θ, the average length of the front end is only a fraction of the entire cache visit. For example, the guestimate (1.6) just suggested in the previous subsection yields a front end which averages one quarter of the entire cache visit. This means that a typical visit to cache consists of a rapid succession of requests, followed by a relatively much longer period in which the track ages out of the cache.

The vast majority of tracks, visiting a real cache, tend to exhibit exactly the pattern of behavior just described. Occasional tracks *can* be found whose use is so persistent that they stay in cache for extended periods, but such tracks tend to make a relatively small contribution to the total time spent in cache by all tracks.

4.2   IMPLICATIONS FOR MEASUREMENT

A simple, easily applied technique exists that makes it possible to estimate the average residency time T, in a running environment, based upon live measurements. To accomplish this, we may proceed by applying Little's law. This fundamental result, widely applied in many areas of performance analysis, was first proved by J. D. C. Little [14]. It states that for any system (where *system* is very broadly defined),

$$\text{population} = \begin{pmatrix} \text{residency} \\ \text{time} \end{pmatrix} \times \begin{pmatrix} \text{arrival} \\ \text{rate} \end{pmatrix} \qquad (1.13)$$

for the averages of these three quantities.

Suppose that measurements are available (as they normally are in a VM or OS/390 environment) for the rate of requests r and the miss ratio m. Let z represent the amount of cache memory occupied by a track, and s represent the total cache size. Then we may conclude that the population of tracks currently visiting the cache is given by (1.13):

$$\frac{s}{z} = rmT \qquad (1.14)$$

Therefore,

$$T = \frac{s}{zrm} \qquad (1.15)$$

By contrast, measurements of the single-reference residency time τ require specific instrumentation that is not available as a part of standard storage subsystem reporting. The comparative ease of measuring the average residency time, and the comparative difficulty of measuring the single-reference residency time, tends to make the former very attractive as a basis for day-to-day capacity planning. Planning based upon the average residency time is investigated further in Chapter 3.

Nevertheless, Computer Associate's CA-ASTEX software package for storage monitoring does include the capability to report the single-reference residency time. The single-reference residency time is also reported, based upon analysis of trace data, by the cache simulation tool called Cache Analysis Aid (CAA). This IBM field diagnostic tool is not offered directly as a product, but IBM storage customers can usually arrange for its use.

By taking advantage of (1.12), it is also possible to estimate the value of θ, for a running workload, given measurements of T and τ:

$$\theta = 1 - \frac{\tau}{T} \qquad (1.16)$$

Another interesting implication of the related equations (1.11) and (1.12) involves determining, from trace data, whether a given track is in cache at the time it is requested. Simulation tools, such as CAA, do this by applying the rules for LRU management to the sequence of requests occurring in the trace.

Let us now consider how to simplify this method of analysis.

One approach is to apply the criterion of time-in-cache. This greatly reduces the amount of information needed about events prior to the current request. Rather than reproducing the entire sequence of cache management actions leading up to the current request, we need only find the previous request made to the same track. The time since this request can then be compared with the single-reference residency time to assess whether the request is a hit or a miss.

Nevertheless, both the approach based upon the criterion of time-in-cache, as well as that based upon LRU list simulation, share a common drawback: their scope of application excludes a substantial period of time at the beginning of the trace. For the former, the time excluded is equal to τ; for the latter, a "warm up" period is needed long enough to fill the simulated cache memory (ordinarily, the length of the "warm up" period is somewhere between τ and T).

The result (1.11) makes possible an entirely different method of analysis. Suppose that the time line is divided into equal intervals $(t_i, t_{i+1}]$, where

$$t_i = i\tau, \qquad i = 0, 1, 2, \ldots$$

If a track is requested at least once during an interval, consider (for purposes of having a convenient term) that the track has been *touched* or, equivalently, that a touch to the track has occurred. Then the "burstiness" of references, together with the fact that no two references during an interval can be separated in time by long enough for a track to age out of cache, imply that:

1. Most touches to a track entail a miss.

2. If a touch *does* entail a miss, then it must be the first I/O to the track during the interval. Any subsequent I/O's must be hits.

Moreover, it is possible to apply (1.11) to quantify the term "most" just used in observation (1) above.

By taking advantage of the fact that most touches entail a miss, it is possible to estimate the number of misses during an interval merely by counting the number of touches (the number of distinct tracks referenced). Since this method uses no information about events in previous intervals, none of the available data must be excluded.

To calculate the probability that a given touch to a track entails a miss, observe that for every miss, there is a corresponding visit to the cache. For each visit, in turn, there is a corresponding back end; and for each back end, there is exactly one *back end I/O* demarking the point where it starts. In addition, an interval cannot contain references from more than one distinct visit; so no more than one miss I/O and no more than one back end I/O can occur in a given interval. Since our objective is to count touches that entail a miss, we may therefore proceed by counting instead touches that entail a back end I/O.

Now, for each interval containing a back end I/O to a given track, there is a corresponding (possibly empty) set of intervals where the track is touched but there is *no* back end I/O. The number of such intervals is given by the number of interval boundaries crossed by the front end (here again we make use of the fact that an interval cannot contain references from more than one distinct visit). Also, every back end lies in exactly two adjacent intervals, thus crossing one interval boundary.

But assuming that the placement of interval boundaries falls at random, the average number of interval boundaries crossed by front ends and by back ends must be in proportion to their durations. Therefore, for each touched interval containing a back end I/O, there must be, on average, $\Delta\tau/\tau$ touched intervals that do not. We may therefore conclude that the probability that a touched interval contains a back end I/O, *and* the probability that a touched interval contains a miss, are both equal to

$$\left[1 + \frac{\Delta\tau}{\tau}\right]^{-1} = 1 - \theta$$

where the expression on the right follows from (1.11).

To apply the conclusion just stated as a method of trace analysis, we count the total number of I/O's n_{req} and touches n_{tch}. We may then estimate

$$m(\tau) \approx (1 - \theta)\frac{n_{tch}}{n_{req}} \qquad (1.17)$$

Note that if θ is in the general ballpark of the guestimate (1.6), then the estimate (1.17) is not highly sensitive to the exact value of θ being assumed. For example, suppose that, in some interval, we count a total of 100,000 references to 20,000 distinct tracks. Then the guestimate (1.6) would yield an estimated hit ratio of $1 - .2 \times (1 - .25) = 85$ percent. By comparison, the alternative assumptions $\theta = .2$ and $\theta = .3$ would yield estimated hit ratios of 84 percent and 86 percent respectively.

4.3   REQUIREMENTS FOR MEMORY

We have just devoted several pages to a detailed discussion of the key, closely related results (1.11) and (1.12), which describe the time spent by a track during a visit to memory. We now derive what is by far the most important consequence of this visit time: the resulting cache memory requirements. We relate these requirements both to the cache miss ratio, as well as to the level of service being provided to applications (as reflected in the average or single-reference residency time).

Our starting point for calculating the requirements for cache memory is Little's law, as applied previously in the result (1.14). The same result can be stated equivalently as

$$s = zrmT \qquad (1.18)$$

By (1.4) and (1.12), we also have

$$m = bT^{-\theta} \qquad (1.19)$$

where

$$b = a(1 - \theta)^{-\theta}$$

Substituting this expression for m into (1.18),

$$s = zbr\,T^{1-\theta} \tag{1.20}$$

In a nutshell, (1.20) says that the requirement for cache memory can be estimated by first establishing an objective for average cache residency time. Reasonable objectives for the average residency time, in turn, can be developed by considering the requirements of individual applications. The next subsection applies and illustrates these ideas.

It is useful to note that the equations (1.4), (1.12), and (1.20) form a "chain" that ties together, in succession, the variables m, τ, T, and s. To summarize the entire "chain" in one place, we have:

$$
\begin{aligned}
m &= a\tau^{-\theta} \\
\tau &= (1-\theta)T \\
T &= \left(\frac{s}{zbr}\right)^{\frac{1}{1-\theta}}
\end{aligned}
\tag{1.21}
$$

where

$$b = a(1-\theta)^{-\theta}$$

All of the relationships just presented are sufficiently simple that it is possible to "skip over" any desired part of the chain through substitution. Also, all of these relationships are easily reversed. For example, if we wish to express the cache size requirements in terms of the single-reference residency time (rather than the average residency time as just studied above) we may reverse the last two equations, then use substitution:

$$
\begin{aligned}
s &= zbr\,T^{1-\theta} \\
&= \frac{zar}{1-\theta}\tau^{1-\theta}
\end{aligned}
\tag{1.22}
$$

As another example, we can use successive substitutions to express the miss ratio as a function of cache size. Just as the miss ratio, as a function of the single-reference residency time, takes the form of a simple power law, so does the miss ratio, as a function of cache memory:

$$
\begin{aligned}
m &= bT^{-\theta} \\
&= b\left(\frac{s}{zbr}\right)^{-\frac{\theta}{1-\theta}}
\end{aligned}
\tag{1.23}
$$

The existence of a power law relationship between these quantities was first noted by Chow [15], and demonstrated convincingly by Smith [16].

When combined with the guestimate (1.6), and applied in a context where there is an existing workload with some known I/O rate, (1.23) yields a useful rule of thumb:

$$m \approx ks^{-1/3} \tag{1.24}$$

for some (not particularly important) constant k. For example, according to the rule of thumb just stated, it is necessary to increase the cache size by eight times, in order to reduce misses by a factor of two.

4.4   AN EMPIRICAL VIEW OF RESIDENCY TIME

As mentioned briefly in introducing the hierarchical reuse model, objectives for the average residency time T can be developed by considering the requirements of individual applications. In view of (1.20), such objectives provide a valuable starting point for configuration planning. Let us, therefore, consider the impact of the average residency time on the performance experienced by a wide range of cached data.

Figures 1.4 through 1.10 present the performance of a "plain vanilla" cache, relative to average residency time, for a range of application storage pools. These include both the VM storage pools already introduced, as well as the storage pools traced during a survey of twelve moderate to large OS/390 installations [17]. The figures include the following OS/390 data pools:

- DB2: On-line DataBase 2 (DB2) database storage.

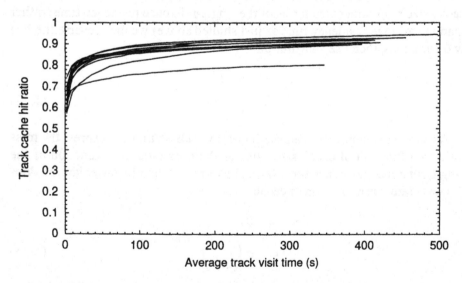

Figure 1.4.   VM user storage pools: cache performance as a function of average cache residency time.

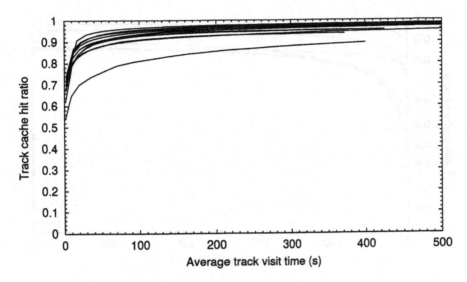

Figure 1.5. VM system storage pools: cache performance as a function of average cache residency time.

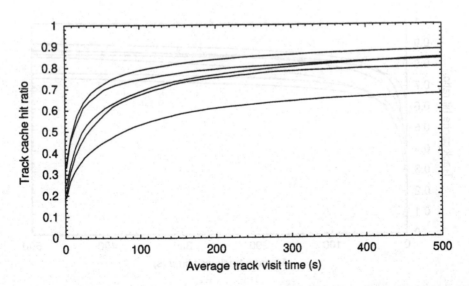

Figure 1.6. DB2 storage pools: cache performance as a function of average cache residency time.

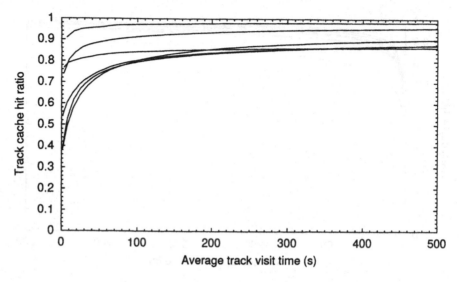

Figure 1.7.   CICS storage pools: cache performance as a function of average cache residency time.

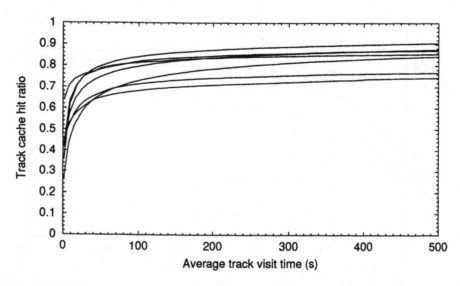

Figure 1.8.   IMS storage pools: cache performance as a function of average cache residency time.

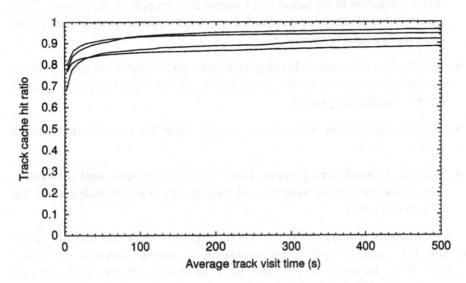

Figure 1.9. TSO storage pools: cache performance as a function of average cache residency time.

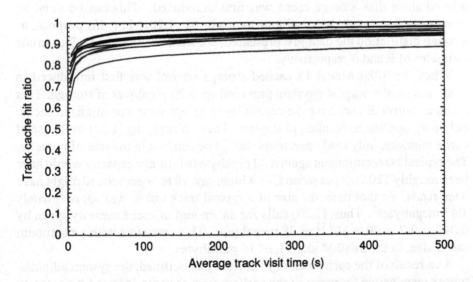

Figure 1.10. OS/390 system storage pools: cache performance as a function of average cache residency time.

- CICS: On-line Virtual Storage Access Method (VSAM) database storage under Customer Information and Control System (CICS) file control. This variety of application accounted for the largest single contribution to the total storage seen in the survey.

- IMS: On-line Information Management System (IMS) database storage (more precisely, storage for databases accessed via the Data Language I (DL/I) database access language).

- TSO: Storage for interactive users running under the Time Sharing Option (TSO).

- System: Control files, program libraries, logs, and data used for system administration (Spool, scratch, and paging data were excluded from the system category).

This author's reading of Figures 1.4 through 1.10 is that, if it is desired to ensure that "cache friendly" applications (at a minimum) receive substantial benefits from the cache, an objective for T of *at least* 30–60 seconds can be recommended. If, in addition, it is desired to get substantial performance gains from applications that are *not* "cache friendly", a more demanding objective may be needed.

The residency time objective of no less than 30 seconds, as just stated, provides an interesting way to assess the cache memory sizes that have been offered since disk storage cache was first introduced. This can be done by comparing them with the requirements given by (1.20). For this purpose, as a rough distillation the data just presented, we shall use 0.25 and 0.7 as crude estimates of θ and b respectively.

When the 3880 Model 13 cached storage control was first introduced in 1982, a typical storage subsystem provided up to 20 gigabytes of storage. That storage control did not have the capability to accept write operations in cache; only read operations resulted in staging. Thus, in applying (1.20) to its use of cache memory, only read operations should be counted in the rate of requests. The typical I/O requirement against 20 gigabytes of storage capacity would have been roughly 120 I/O's per second, of which, say, 90 I/O's per second might have been reads. At that time, the size of a typical track image was approximately .047 megabytes[1]. Thus, (1.20) calls for an amount of cache memory given by $0.047 \times 0.7 \times 90 \times 30^{0.75} = 38$ megabytes. This compares with a maximum cache size, in the 3880 Model 13, of 16 megabytes.

As a result of the cache memory shortfall just outlined, the system administrators responsible for many of the earliest storage controls found it necessary to carefully manage the use of cache storage. Cached storage controls were deployed selectively, for use with "cache friendly" data. Also, extensive use was made of the facilities provided in these storage controls for limiting the use of cache memory to identified volumes, while "turning off" access to the cache by other volumes.

Cache sizes increased sharply with the introduction of the 3880 Model 23 storage control (maximum cache size 64 megabytes), and again with the 3990 Model 3 storage control (maximum cache size 256 megabytes). At the beginning of the 1990's, a typical storage control was configured with approximately 120 gigabytes of storage capacity, and an I/O demand of, say, 300 I/O's per second. Both reads and writes were cached. By this time, memory management techniques had improved so that, when staging data as the result of a miss, it was possible to allocate only enough memory for the requested record and subsequent records on the track (if a request then occurred for data before the requested record, a fairly unusual event, this would cause a so-called "front-end miss"). Thus, the size of the most common track image at this time was 0.057 megabytes[2], but we shall assume $z = 0.04$ megabytes (the approximate memory allocation required, on average, for a stage). During this time, (1.20) would suggest that a typical storage control should have been configured with $0.04 \times 0.7 \times 300 \times 30^{0.75} = 108$ megabytes of cache memory. However, storage controls were often configured with less, since such memory was still fairly expensive. Many installations adopted 64 megabytes as their standard cache size. At this time, the use of explicit controls to restrict the use of cache memory remained common.

Today, storage controls offer far larger amounts of memory. Most models of storage control, for use in a OS/390 environment, cannot be purchased with less than 1–2 gigabytes of cache. A typical storage control might be configured with one terrabyte of storage capacity, and an I/O demand of, say, 1000 I/O's per second. Such storage control configurations typically have more than enough cache, by the standards just discussed in the previous paragraph.

Let us continue to assume that $z = 0.04$ megabytes (as before, this represents the approximate average memory required to stage the contents of a standard track image, from the requested record to the end of the track). Then using the typical configuration just suggested, (1.20) calls for a cache size of $0.04 \times 0.7 \times 1000 \times 30^{0.75} = 359$ megabytes. This requirement is likely to be less than the configurable minimum size by a factor of several times. Due to the fact that cache sizes today are so much more generous than those typical ten years ago, there now tends to be little or no use of strategies to explicitly control access to cache memory.

In capacity planning for storage control cache, however, a more demanding objective must be adopted today than the minimal level of service obtained using $T = 30$ seconds. This is not only because more demanding objectives are easily achievable, but also because they *are* being achieved, day to day, by running applications. Very high standards of cache performance are both routine, and expected.

In moving an application from an older storage control to a newer one, the system administrator is well advised to keep an eye on the average cache residency time being delivered to applications, in order to avoid placing current service level agreements at risk. This can be done using cache performance measurements which are standard in VM and OS/390 environments, together with the estimates of the average cache residency time presented previously in Subsection 4.2.

4.5   SEQUENTIAL WORKLOADS

While on the subject of residency time objectives, it is appropriate to include a brief discussion of *sequential* workloads. Sequential work plays an important role in batch processing, particularly during off-shift hours. The characteristics and requirements of sequential I/O contrast sharply with those of random-access I/O, and in general sequential work must be analyzed as a special case, rather than using the same probabilistic or statistical methods that apply to a random-access environment.

The next request for a given item of *sequential* data tends to be either immediate, or a relatively long time in the future. As a result, most cached storage controls perform *early demotion* of sequential data residing in the cache; the memory for such data is typically freed long before the data would have progressed from the top to the bottom of the LRU list. Storage controls also typically use *sequential prestage* operations to bring data that appears to be due for sequential processing into cache in advance of anticipated requests. The net result of sequential prestage, coupled with early demotion, is that sequential processing tends to exhibit very high hit ratios and very light use of cache memory.

When both sequential prestage and early demotion are being performed by the controller, tracks entering the cache via prestage are normally granted a much shorter cache visit time compared with tracks being staged due to a miss. For this reason, it is impractical to specify a residency time objective for sequential work, nor is such an objective necessary to achieve good sequential performance.

Due to the high hit ratios and light memory use characteristic of sequential processing, sequential workloads do not usually interfere with the practical analysis of cache memory requirements based upon Little's law. For example, (1.15) can still be applied to estimate the average residency time of the cache, even when sequential work is present. For this purpose, only true misses, not sequential prestage operations, should be included in computing the miss ratio. This limits the scope of Little's law (the system "population") to those tracks that age out of cache normally; hence, it yields an estimated average time for normal (rather than sequential) cache visits. The small use of cache memory due to sequential tracks causes an upward error in the estimate, but this error tends to be minor due to the light memory requirements for sequential processing.

5. TWO LEVELS OF CACHE

So far, despite our interest in a wide range of storage pools on both VM and OS/390 systems, we have examined interarrival statistics on VM systems only. This is due to the more complex nature of file buffering in OS/390. By contrast with the case for VM, *any* I/O trace collected in a production OS/390 environment is likely to reflect the presence of file buffers in the processor. Therefore, before examining interarrival data obtained in this environment, it is necessary to consider what impact should be expected from such buffers.

It is not so much the performance of the processor buffers *themselves* which complicate the picture developed so far, since their performance can be described by the methods of analysis already discussed. Instead, it is necessary to examine the impact that processor buffering has on the I/O requests being made to the storage subsystem.

Typically, write requests issued by OS/390 applications result in update operations in *both* the processor buffer area *and* the storage subsystem, since it is necessary to ensure that the new information will be permanently retained (the new data must be *hardened*). One copy of the data, however, is sufficient to satisfy a read request. For this reason, we must expect some read hits to occur only in the processor, which otherwise would have occurred in storage control cache.

The effect of this on the cache miss ratio is easiest to see when the single-reference residency time in the processor is shorter than that in the cache, i.e., when $\tau_c \geq \tau_p$, where the subscripts c and p are used to denote processor and storage control cache memories, respectively. In this case, all the hits in the processor overlap with hits that would have occurred in the cache by itself, assuming that the cache's single-reference residency time is held fixed. The effect of processor buffering is, therefore, to reduce the number of requests to the cache without any reduction in cache misses. For reads, we should therefore expect that

$$m'_c(\tau_c) \approx \frac{m_c(\tau_c)}{m_p(\tau_p)} \qquad (1.25)$$

where the prime indicates the miss ratio in the combined configuration.

A more interesting configuration is one in which $\tau_c < \tau_p$. In this environment, a "division of labor" becomes possible, in which the processor buffer provides long residency times, while the storage control cache provides additional hits by storing entire track images rather than individual records. The analysis of this case is more complex, but it can be shown in this case also that the miss ratio for reads in the cache, with processor buffers also present, can be estimated as a function of the miss ratios for the two memory technologies operating separately [18]:

$$m'_c(\tau_c) \approx \frac{m_c(\tau_c)}{m_p(\tau_c)} \tag{1.26}$$

(Note, in applying (1.26), that the processor miss ratio must be evaluated at the single-reference residency time of the storage control cache).

Plugging (1.4) into (1.26), we find that, for reads, in the case $\tau_c < \tau_p$,

$$m'(\tau_c) \approx \frac{a_c}{a_p}\tau_c^{-(\theta_c-\theta_p)} \tag{1.27}$$

Since the management of processor buffers is at the level of individual application records (typically one page in size), we may assume that $\theta_p < \theta_c$. Thus, the behavior of the cache under these conditions is analogous to the simpler case when no processor buffers are present, except that a negative exponent with a smaller absolute value, $-(\theta_c - \theta_p)$, appears in place of $-\theta_c$.

Since (1.27) bears such a close resemblance to (1.4), virtually the entire line of reasoning presented in the previous subsections extends to the case of reads to a cache, where processor buffers are present. Corresponding to (1.21), we obtain

$$
\begin{aligned}
m'_c &\approx \frac{a_c}{a_p}\tau_c^{-(\theta_c-\theta_p)} \\
\tau_c &\approx [1 - (\theta_c - \theta_p)]T'_c \\
T'_c &\approx \left(\frac{s_c}{z_c b'_c m_p r}\right)^{\frac{1}{1-(\theta_c-\theta_p)}}
\end{aligned}
\tag{1.28}
$$

where

$$b'_c = \frac{a_c}{a_p}[1 - (\theta_c - \theta_p)]^{-(\theta_c-\theta_p)}$$

provided that $\tau_c < \tau_p$.

What form, then, should a plot such as that presented by Figure 1.2 take, if processor buffers are present? In the region of the plot corresponding to $\tau_c \geq \tau_p$, (1.25) shows that the slope of the plot should be unchanged; it will merely shift due to division by a constant. In the region $\tau_c < \tau_p$, however, the plot should show reduced responsiveness, reflecting the reduced exponent appearing in (1.27).

Also, the transition between the two regions of the curve will reflect the processor buffering that is being applied to the applications within the storage pool. If no processor buffers are present, or if the processor buffer area is very small, then we should expect to see no transition (instead, we should see a single straight line). If processor buffering is present, but varies significantly between individual applications, we should expect to see a gradual transition.

If processor buffering is applied consistently, with the same value of τ_p across the entire storage pool, we should expect to see a sharp transition at the point where the single-reference residency time of the cache assumes this value.

The expected performance of a cache managed at the record (rather than track) level is similar to that just discussed, in that it is necessary to distinguish between the two regimes $\tau_c < \tau_p$ and $\tau_c \geq \tau_p$. For a record-managed cache, however, the disparity between the two regimes will be sharper. Essentially *no* hits in storage control cache should be expected for read requests with record interarrival times shorter than τ_p, since in this case the needed record should always be available in a file buffer.

Taking a step back, we can now observe that, although the discussion of the previous several paragraphs began by examining two specific levels of the memory hierarchy, we might just as easily have been talking about *any* two such levels, one of which lies immediately below the other. In view of this broader context, let us again review our conclusions.

Assuming that the upper of two adjacent memory levels obeys the hierarchical reuse model, the performance of the lower level, as a function of single-reference residency time, is likely to contain a transition region. Nevertheless, the mathematical model (1.4), with suitable calibration of θ and a, can still be used to produce a serviceable approximation of the miss ratios in the lower memory level, *away from the transition region*. In order for the application of (1.4) to be sound, there must, however, be a substantial difference in residency times between the two levels.

In the traditional view of a memory hierarchy, the size, and hence the residency time, of each layer increases sharply compared to the layer above it. Within this framework, we may conclude that if (1.4) applies at any one level of the hierarchy, it should also apply at all of the levels below. Therefore, there is no contradiction in adopting the hierarchical reuse model as a method of approximating data reference at *all* levels of a traditional memory hierarchy.

In Chapter 4, we shall argue, in some cases, for the reverse of the traditional framework: a residency time in the processor buffer area which substantially exceeds that in storage control cache. In such cases also, we should anticipate that (1.4) will provide a practical model of the resulting cache performance, due to the large difference between the cache and processor file buffer residency times.

5.1 COMPARISON WITH EMPIRICAL DATA

Figures 1.11 through 1.20 present the actual interarrival statistics observed at the 12 large OS/390 installations just introduced in the previous section. These figures largely conform to the expectations just outlined in the previous paragraphs. The plots for the DB2, CICS, and IMS storage pools show reduced responsiveness at low single-reference residency times, and turn upward as the

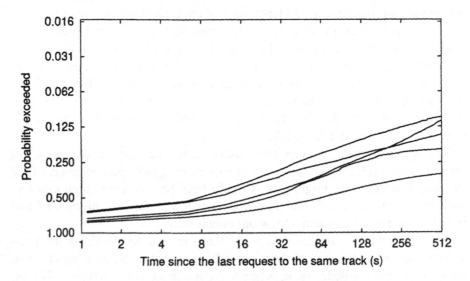

Figure 1.11.   DB2 storage pools: distribution of track interarrival times.

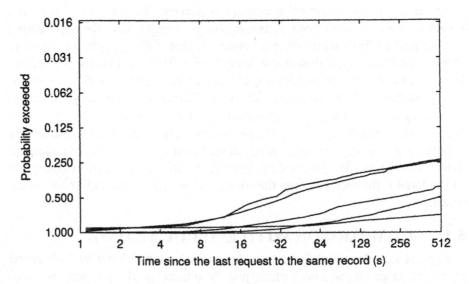

Figure 1.12.   DB2 storage pools: distribution of record interarrival times.

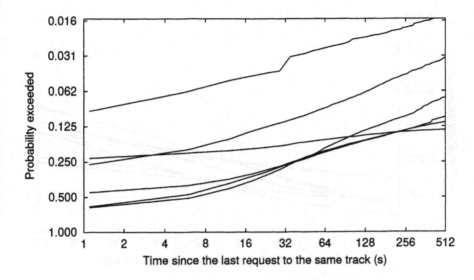

Figure 1.13. CICS storage pools: distribution of track interarrival times.

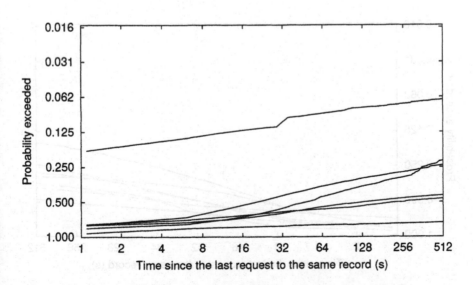

Figure 1.14. CICS storage pools: distribution of record interarrival times.

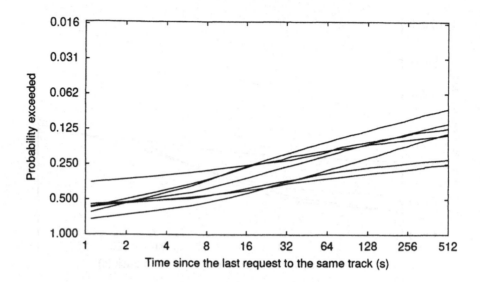

Figure 1.15.   IMS storage pools: distribution of track interarrival times.

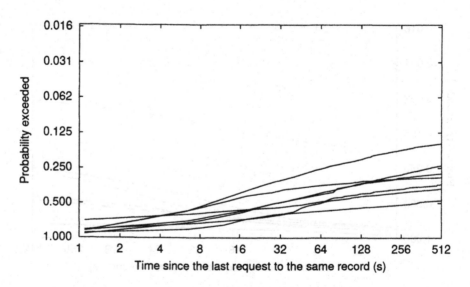

Figure 1.16.   IMS storage pools: distribution of record interarrival times.

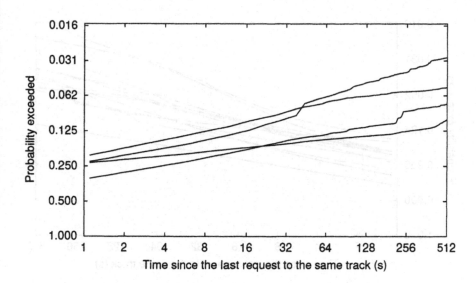

Figure 1.17.   TSO storage pools: distribution of track interarrival times.

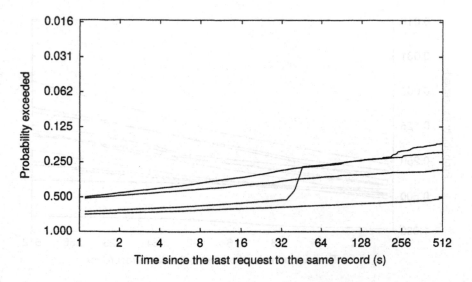

Figure 1.18.   TSO storage pools: distribution of record interarrival times.

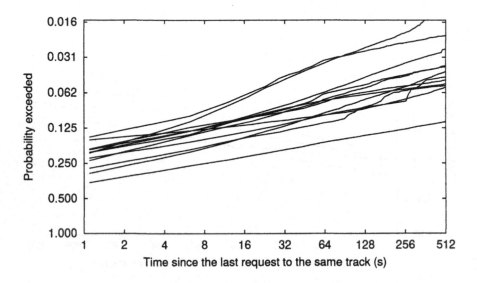

Figure 1.19.   OS/390 system storage pools: distribution of track interarrival times.

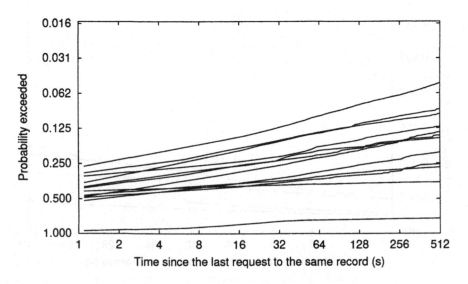

Figure 1.20.   OS/390 system storage pools: distribution of record interarrival times.

single-reference residency time lengthens. Thus, as we should expect, these plots suggest an important role for processor file buffers in the production database storage pools.

In Chapters 3 and 5, we shall sometimes adopt a mathematical model in which multiple workloads share the same cache or processor buffer area, and each individual workload conforms to the hierarchical reuse model. This results in a series of equations of the form (1.5), one for each workload. In graphical terms, it corresponds to fitting each workload's plot of interarrival statistics with a straight line.

Collectively, Figures 1.2, 1.3, and 1.11 through 1.20 provide the justification for adopting the mathematical model just described. The *multiple workload hierarchical reuse model*, as just outlined in the previous paragraph, is both sufficiently simple, and sufficiently realistic, to provide a practical framework for examining how to get the most out of a cache shared by multiple, distinct workloads.

Notes

1 Assumes a track belonging to the 3380 family of storage devices.
2 Assumes a track belonging to the 3390 family of storage devices.

Chapter 2

HIERARCHICAL REUSE DAEMON

To conduct realistic performance benchmarks of storage subsystem performance, one attractive approach is to construct the required benchmark driver out of building blocks that resemble, as closely as possible, actual applications or users running in a realistic environment. This chapter develops a simple "toy" version of an application whose pattern of reference conforms to the hierarchical reuse model. Such a toy application can be implemented as an independently executing "daemon" [19], and provides a natural building block for I/O performance testing. In addition, it helps bring to life, in the form of a concrete example, the hierarchical reuse model itself.

It is reasonably simple to implement a toy application of the form that we shall present, and to test its cache behavior directly against the characteristics of the hierarchical reuse model. Nevertheless, this chapter also provides a crude, asymptotic analysis to explain why we should expect the comparison to be a favorable one.

To accomplish the needed analysis, we must first put the behavior of the hierarchical reuse model into a form convenient for comparison against the proposed toy application. With this background in place, we then propose, and analyze, a method by which it is possible to match this behavior synthetically. Finally, we illustrate the actual behavior of the proposed synthetic requests through simulation.

1.   DESIRED BEHAVIOR

Assuming that a pattern of requests obeys the hierarchical reuse model, consider the expected arrival rate $\lambda(t)$, to a specific track, after an amount of time t has passed since some given I/O request. The behavior of $\lambda(t)$ provides an alternative method of characterizing the hierarchical reuse model, which proves to be useful for comparison against the proposed synthetic pattern of requests.

To estimate $\lambda(t)$, assume that some initial request occurs at time $t = 0$ (time is measured relative to whatever initial request we choose to examine). Consider the number $N(t)$ of requests that occur at some time $0 < t_i \leq t$.

Let us now assume that the I/O requests are being serviced by a cache, whose single-reference residency time is given by $\tau = t$. To determine the expectation of $N(t)$, we must examine all potential choices of the initial I/O request. Let us divide these potential choices into groups, depending upon the cache visit within which they occur.

For any given, initial I/O request, let $V(t)$ be the largest number of I/O's that occurs during any time period of length t that falls within the cache visit that contains the request. Note that $V(t)$ is identical for all initial I/O requests that fall within the same cache visit. Also, for all such I/O's, $0 \leq N(t) \leq V(t) - 1$ (the case $N(t) = V(t)$ cannot occur since the count of I/O's given by $N(t)$ does not include the I/O at time $t = 0$). Moreover, values must occur throughout this range, including both extremes. For the identified cache visit, we therefore adopt the rough estimate $E[N(t)] \approx \frac{1}{2}[V(t) - 1]$. For *all* cache visits, we estimate that

$$E[N(t)] \approx \frac{1}{2}\{E[V(t)] - 1\}$$

But the expected number of I/O's per cache visit is just $1/m(t)$. Although not all of these must necessarily occur during any single time period of length t, such an outcome is fairly likely due to the tendency of I/O's to come in bursts. Thus, $E[V(t)] \approx 1/m(t)$, which implies

$$E[N(t)] \approx \frac{1}{2}\left[\frac{1}{m(t)} - 1\right]$$

Asymptotically, for sufficiently small miss ratios,

$$E[N(t)] \approx \frac{1}{2m(t)} = \frac{1}{2a}t^{\theta} \tag{2.1}$$

Based upon (2.1), we can now state the asymptotic behavior of the arrival rate $\lambda(t)$. For sufficiently small miss ratios, we have

$$\begin{aligned} \lambda(t) &= \frac{d}{dt}E[N(t)] \\ &\approx \frac{\theta}{2a}t^{\theta-1} \end{aligned} \tag{2.2}$$

This is the asymptotic behavior that we wish to emulate.

2. DEFINITION OF THE SYNTHETIC APPLICATION

We now define a synthetic, toy application that performs a random walk within a defined range of tracks. A number of tracks equal to a power of two are assumed to be available for use by the application, which are labeled with the track numbers $0 \le l \le 2^{H_{max}} - 1$. In the limit, as the number of available tracks is allowed to grow sufficiently large, we shall show that the pattern of references reproduces the asymptotic behavior stated by (2.2).

The method of performing the needed random walk can be visualized by thinking of the available tracks as being the leaves of a binary tree, of height H_{max}. The ancestors of any given track number l are identified implicitly by the binary representation of the number l. For example, suppose that $H_{max} = 3$. Then any of the eight available track numbers l can be represented as a three-digit binary number. The parent of any track l, in turn, can be represented as a two digit binary number, obtained by dropping the last binary digit of the number l; the grandparent can be represented as a one digit binary number, obtained by dropping the last two binary digits of the number l; and all tracks have the same great-grandparent.

Starting from a given leaf l_i of the tree, the next leaf l_{i+1} is determined as follows. First, climb a number of nodes $0 \le k \ll H_{max}$ above leaf l_i. Then, with probability v, climb one node higher; with another probability of v, climb an additional node higher; and so on (but stop at the top of the tree). Finally, select a leaf at random from all of those belonging to the subtree under the current node.

No special data structure is needed to implement the random tree-climbing operation just described. Instead, it is only necessary to calculate the random height $0 \le H \le H_{max}$ at which climbing terminates. The next track is then given by the formula

$$l_{i+1} = 2^H \left\lfloor \frac{l_i}{2^H} \right\rfloor + \lfloor R\,2^H \rfloor$$

where R is a uniformly distributed random number in the range $0 \le R < 1$.

3. ANALYSIS OF THE SYNTHETIC APPLICATION

Consider, now, the probability of a repeat request occurring to track l_i, at step $i + n$ (the nth step after some identified initial request i). Suppose that $H_{highest}$ (abbreviated H_{hi}) is the maximum of the heights H encountered in producing the requests $i + 1, \ldots, i + n$, and that this maximum height was encountered in producing the request $i < i + n_{hi} \le i + n$. Then clearly, track l_i is one of the leaves in the subtree from which the random selection at step $i + n_{hi}$ is performed.

Moreover, given no further information as to events occurring at steps $i + n_{hi}$ or after, any of the leaves of this subtree might be selected at step $i + n$, and these are the only leaves that can be selected. By symmetry, it follows that the probability of a repeat request to track l_i, at step $i + n$, is identical to the probability of requesting any other leaf of the same subtree, namely $2^{-H_{hi}}$. Putting the same fact in a different way, it is the lowest value of 2^{-H} achieved in n trials of the random variable H.

To understand the implications of this, consider, first, a *single* trial. We now wish to determine the cumulative distribution $F(\cdot)$ of the quantity 2^{-H}. This is a step function, since H assumes only discrete values. For the present purpose, it suffices to consider only the values of the domain of $F(\cdot)$ that have non-zero probabilities. Let $H = k + j$; that is, $j \geq 0$ represents the random part of H after removing the constant k. Also, let us assume that the upper bound on j, imposed by the height H_{max} of the tree's root, is sufficiently large that its presence can be neglected. Then, by taking advantage of the fact that j is distributed as a geometric random variable with parameter ν, we have

$$
\begin{aligned}
F(2^{-(k+j)}) &= \sum_{i=0}^{\infty}(1 - \nu)\nu^{j+i} \\
&= (1 - \nu)\nu^j \sum_{i=0}^{\infty} \nu^i \\
&= \nu^j
\end{aligned}
\tag{2.3}
$$

Given this description of $F(\cdot)$, we may apply the David-Johnson extreme value approximation [20] to estimate the smallest value γ_{hi} of the random variable $\gamma = 2^{-H}$ which we should expect after n trials. To obtain the needed estimate, this technique requires us to solve the equation

$$
F(\gamma_{hi}) = \frac{1}{n + 1}
\tag{2.4}
$$

Since γ_{hi} assumes only discrete values, (2.4) cannot, in general, be solved exactly. In many applications of the David-Johnson approximation, a complication of this type must be dealt with carefully. For our own purpose, however, we choose to disregard the requirement that the solution must be discrete, since we are not so much interested in obtaining a precise solution for any given value of n, as we are in determining the asymptotic behavior of the solution as n increases.

Keeping in mind that a given value of γ_{hi} has a corresponding highest climb $H_{hi} = j_{hi} + k$, and that $j_{hi} = H_{hi} - k = -\log_2 \gamma_{hi} - k$, we may take advantage of (2.3) to express (2.4) equivalently as

$$
\nu^{-\log_2 \gamma_{hi} - k} = \frac{1}{n + 1}
$$

This equation is easily solved to yield,

$$\gamma_{hi} = [(n+1)v^{-k}]^{1/\log_2 v} \tag{2.5}$$

We can now return to the behavior of the arrival rate $\lambda(t)$. To introduce time into our synthetic framework for generating requests, we set $n = tr$, where r represents the number of synthetic requests per second which we wish to produce. Based upon (2.5), we must then have that the arrival rate of a repeat request, which follows an initial request by an amount of time t, is given by

$$\lambda'(t) = r\gamma_{hi} = r[(tr+1)v^{-k}]^{1/\log_2 v}$$

or asymptotically,

$$\lambda'(t) = r^{1+1/\log_2 v} v^{-k/\log_2 v} t^{1/\log_2 v} \tag{2.6}$$

Comparing (2.2) with (2.6), we can therefore arrange matters so that, asymptotically, $\lambda'(t) = \lambda(t)$. This requires that the two conditions

$$\theta - 1 = \frac{1}{\log_2 v}$$

and

$$\frac{\theta}{2a} = r^{1+1/\log_2 v} v^{-k/\log_2 v}$$

be met. Simplifying, these two conditions yield the parameter values

$$v = 2^{-1/(1-\theta)} \tag{2.7}$$

and

$$k = -\frac{\ln(\theta/(2a))}{\ln 2} + \left[\frac{1}{\ln v} + \frac{1}{\ln 2} \right] \ln r \tag{2.8}$$

In view of the rough nature of the calculations just presented, and since k must be a small integer, it should not be surprising that, in practice, k is best determined by trial and error, rather than by direct application of (2.8). Experiments performed via simulation show that it is easy to select parameters k and v which result in a pattern of reference that faithfully conforms to the hierarchical reuse model, not just asymptotically, but throughout the behavioral range of interest.

4.   EMPIRICAL BEHAVIOR

Figures 2.1, 2.2, and 2.3 present the results of a series of simulation experiments. Each test was performed with a simulated request rate of one I/O per second. To reflect a range of values for the parameter θ, tests were performed for $\nu = 0.44$ (corresponding to $\theta = 0.15$), $\nu = 0.40$ (corresponding to $\theta = 0.25$), and $\nu = 0.34$ (corresponding to $\theta = 0.35$). Each figure shows the results for a specific value of ν, and also the slope θ that, by (2.7), should correspond to that value. For each value of the parameter ν, the cases $k = 0$ through $k = 3$ are examined. All simulations used the value $H_{max} = 14$ (a high enough value to prevent this limit from having a noticeable impact).

A strong match is apparent between the curves presented by Figures 2.1–2.3 and the intended characteristics. Many of the curves appear to be, not just asymptotically linear, but linear throughout the entire range of the plot. If we focus specifically on the most interesting region of interarrival times (those in the range of 32–512 seconds), all of the curves appear to have settled into a close approximation of the predicted asymptotic slope throughout this range.

The figures do show a slight dependency of the slope upon the parameter k, which is not predicted by the analysis presented in the previous section, and which becomes stronger as k increases. It is possible that this dependency may disappear for extremely large values of the interarrival time, or it may reflect a second-order effect not captured by the approximate method of analysis adopted in the previous section.

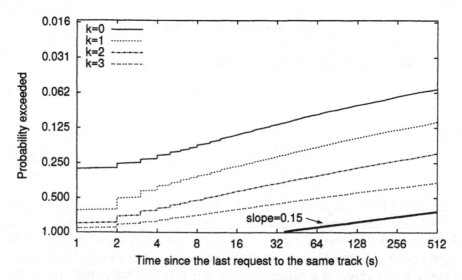

Figure 2.1.   Distribution of interarrival times for a synthetic application running at one request per second, with $\nu = 0.44$ (corresponding to $\theta = 0.15$).

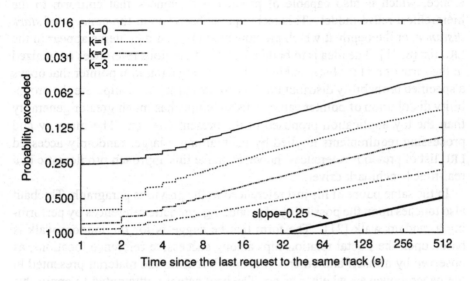

Figure 2.2. Distribution of interarrival times for a synthetic application running at one request per second, with $\nu = 0.40$ (corresponding to $\theta = 0.25$).

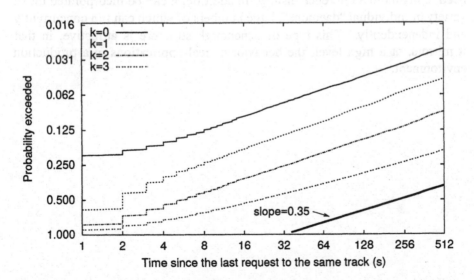

Figure 2.3. Distribution of interarrival times for a synthetic application running at one request per second, with $\nu = 0.34$ (corresponding to $\theta = 0.35$).

A general-purpose technique exists for generating synthetic patterns of reference, which is also capable of producing references that conform to the hierarchical reuse model. This technique is based upon the concept of *stack distance*, or the depth at which previously referenced data items appear in the LRU list [8, 21]. The idea is to build a history of previous references (organized in the form of an LRU list), and index into it using a random pointer that obeys a specified probability distribution. Due to the ability to manipulate the probability distribution of pointer values, this technique has much greater generality than the toy application proposed in the present chapter. The memory and processing requirements implied by maintaining a large, randomly accessed LRU list of previous references, however, make this approach problematic in a real-time benchmark driver.

In the same paper of his just referenced in the previous paragraph, Thiébaut also touches upon the possibility of producing synthetic references by performing a random walk [21]. The form that he suggests for the random walk is based upon the fractal relationships among successive reference locations, as observed by himself and others. It is not clear from the material presented in the paper, however, whether or not Thiébaut actually attempted to apply this idea, or what results he might have obtained.

Returning to the context of the hierarchical reuse model, we have shown that its behavior can, in fact, be produced by a specific form of random walk. The proposed random walk technique has the important advantage that there is no need to maintain a reference history. In addition, it can be incorporated into a variety of individual "daemons", large numbers of which can run concurrently and independently. This type of benchmark structure is attractive, in that it mirrors, at a high level, the behavior of real applications in a production environment.

Chapter 3

USE OF MEMORY BY MULTIPLE WORKLOADS

The opening chapter of the book urges the system administrator responsible for storage performance to keep an eye on the average residency time currently being delivered to applications. In an installation that must meet high standards of storage performance, however, the strategy suggested by this advice may be too passive. To take a proactive role in managing application performance, it is necessary for the storage administrator to be able to examine, not just cache residency times, but also the amounts of cache memory used by each application. This information, for example, makes it possible to ensure that the cache size of a new storage control is adequate to support the applications planned for it. The purpose of the present chapter is to develop a simple and powerful "back-of-the-envelope" calculation of cache use by individual applications.

The proposed technique is based on a key simplifying assumption, which we shall adopt as a

Working hypothesis: *Whether an application is by itself in a cache or shares the cache, its hit ratio can be projected as a function of the average cache residency time for the cache as a whole. Except for this relationship, its performance can be projected independently of any other pools served by the cache.*

In the first subsection of the chapter, we examine this hypothesis more closely. It leads directly to the needed analysis of cache use by individual applications.

To motivate the hypothesis just stated, recall that all workloads sharing a cache share the same, common single-reference residency time τ. The effect of the working hypothesis is to proceed as though the same were true, not just for the single-reference residency time, but for the average residency time as well.

In the usual process for cache capacity planning, the bottom line is to develop *overall* requirements for cache memory, and *overall* expectations for the corresponding hit ratio. The practical usefulness of the proposed working hypothesis thus rests on its ability to yield accurate hit ratio estimates for the configured cache *as a whole*.

The final subsection of the chapter compares overall cache hit ratio estimates, obtained using the working hypothesis, with more precise estimates that might have been obtained using the hierarchical reuse model. We show that, despite variations in residency time among applications, the working hypothesis yields a sound first-order estimate of the overall hit ratio. Thus, although the working hypothesis is admittedly a simplifying approximation, strong grounds can be offered upon which to justify it.

1.   CACHE USE BY APPLICATION

Suppose that some identified application i comprises the *entire* workload on a cache. Then we may conclude, as a direct application of (1.18), that

$$s_i = z_i r_i m_i T \tag{3.1}$$

where the subscripts i denote quantities that refer specifically to application i. The central consequence of the working hypothesis just introduced is that, *as a simplifying approximation, we choose to proceed as though the same result were also true in a cache shared by a mix of applications.*

For example, suppose that it is desired to configure cache memory for a new OS/390 storage subsystem that will be used to contain a mix of three applications: a point of sale (POS) application implemented with CICS/VSAM, an Enterprise Resource Planning (ERP) database implemented with DB2, and storage for 20 application developers running on TSO. Then, as a starting point, we can examine the current requirements of the same applications.

Tables 3.1–3.3 present a set of hypothetical data and analysis that could be developed using standard performance reports. Data assembled for this purpose should normally be obtained at times that represent peak-load conditions.

In the example of the figures, the ERP and TSO applications both currently share a single cache (belonging to the storage subsystem with volume addresses starting at 1F00); the POS application uses a different cache (belonging to the storage subsystem with volume addresses starting at 0880). The average residency time for each cache is calculated by applying (1.15) to the total cache workload, as presented by Table 3.1. For example, the average residency time for the cache belonging to the storage subsystem with volume addresses starting at 0880 is calculated as $1024/(.04 \times 425 \times .23) = 262$ seconds.

We proceed by assuming that this average residency time applies both to the cache as a whole (Table 3.1) as well as to each application currently contained in it (Table 3.2). Based upon this assumption, we may then apply (1.18) to calculate the current cache use of each application. For example, the current cache use of the ERP application is calculated as $.04 \times 490 \times .36 \times 197 = 1390$ megabytes. The total current cache use of the three applications is 1891 megabytes; their aggregate hit ratio (average hit ratio, weighted by I/O rate) is calculated as $(230 \times .81 + 490 \times .64 + 50 \times .89)/770 = .71$.

We must now decide upon an objective for the average residency time of the target system. To ensure that all applications experience equal or better performance, a reasonable choice is to adopt the longest average residency time among the three applications (262 seconds) as the objective. Table 3.3 presents the estimated performance of the three applications, assuming this objective for

Storage Subsystem Starting Address (Hex)	Cache Size (MB)	Stage Size (MB)	I/O Rate per s	Total Hit Ratio	Average Residency Time (s)
0880	1024	.04	425	.77	262
1F00	2048	.04	840	.69	197

Table 3.1.   Cache planning example: current storage subsystems.

Application	Storage Subsystem Starting Address (Hex)	Average Residency Time (s)	Stage Size (MB)	I/O Rate per s	Total Hit Ratio	Cache Use (MB)
POS	0880	262	.04	230	.81	458
ERP	1F00	197	.04	490	.64	1390
TSO	1F00	197	.04	50	.89	43
All				770	.71	1891

Table 3.2.   Cache planning example: three applications contained in current storage.

Application	Storage Subsystem Starting Address (Hex)	Average Residency Time (s)	Stage Size (MB)	I/O Rate per s	Total Hit Ratio	Cache Use (MB)
POS	New	262	.04	230	.81	458
ERP	New	262	.04	490	.66	1746
TSO	New	262	.04	50	.90	52
All	New	262	.04	770	.72	2256

Table 3.3.   Cache planning example: target environment for the same three applications.

the average residency time. The adjusted hit ratios are obtained by applying the proportionality relationship expressed by (1.19), with $\theta = .25$; for example, the miss ratio for the ERP application is projected as $.36 \times (262/197)^{-.25} = .34$. Based upon the projected residency times and hit ratios, we may then compute the cache storage requirements, as already discussed for the previous table. In this way, we obtain an objective of 2256 megabytes for the cache size of the target system. If these requirements could be met exactly, then we would project an aggregate hit ratio, for the three applications, of 72 percent.

As a final step, we must also consider how to round off the computed cache memory requirement of 2256 megabytes. Since this requirement is very close to 2 gigabytes, we might choose, in this case, to round down rather than up. Alternatively, it would also be reasonable to round up to, say, 3 gigabytes, on the grounds that the additional cache can be used for growth in the workload. To account for the rounding off of cache memory, we can apply the proportionality expressed by (1.23). Thus, after rounding down to 2 gigabytes, we would expect the aggregate miss ratio of the target system to be $.28 \times (2048/2256)^{-.25/.75} = .29$, identical to the current aggregate miss ratio of the three applications.

If the available performance reporting tools are sufficiently complete, it is possible to refine the methods presented in the preceding example. In the figures of the example, the stage size was assumed to be equal to .04 megabytes (a reasonable approximation for most OS/390 workloads). The capability to support direct measurements of this quantity has recently been incorporated into some storage controls; if such measurements are supported, they can be found in the System Measurement Facility (SMF) record type 74, subtype 5.

Also, in the example, we used the total miss ratio as our measure of the percentage of I/O's that require more cache memory to be allocated. A loophole exists in this technique, however, due to the capability of most current storage controls to accept write requests without needing to wait for a stage to occur. In a storage control of this type, virtually all write requests will typically be reported as "hits," even though some of them may require allocation of memory. For database I/O, this potential source of error is usually not important, since write requests tend to be updates of data already in cache. If, however, it is desired to account for any write "hits" that may nevertheless require allocation of cache memory, counts of these can also be found in SMF record type 74, subtype 5 (they are called write *promotions*).

Finally, we assumed the guestimate $\theta = .25$. If measurements of the single-reference residency time are available, then θ can be quantified more precisely using (1.16).

2.   ANALYSIS OF THE WORKING HYPOTHESIS

It is beyond the scope of the present chapter to analyze rigorously *every* potential source of error in a capacity planning exercise of the type just presented in the previous section, nor does a "back of the envelope" approximation method require this. Instead, we now focus on the following claim, central to applications of the working hypothesis: that it makes very little difference in the estimated hit ratio of the cache as a whole, whether the individual workloads within the cache are modeled with their correct average residency times, or whether they all are modeled assuming a common average residency time reflecting the conditions for the cache as a whole.

Obviously, such a statement cannot hold *in all cases*. Instead, it is a statement about the realistic impact of typical variations between workloads. As the data presented in Chapter 1 suggests, the values of the parameter θ, for distinct workloads within a given environment, often vary over a fairly narrow range. This gives the proposed hypothesis an important head start, since the hypothesis would be exactly correct for a cache in which several workloads share the same value of the parameter θ. In that case, the common value of θ, together with the fact that all the workloads must share a common single reference residency time τ, would then imply, by (1.12), that the workloads must also the same average residency time as well.

Consider, now, a cache whose activity can be described by the multiple workload hierarchical reuse model; that is, the cache provides service to n individual workloads, $i = 1, 2, \ldots, n$, each of which can be described by the hierarchical reuse model. The true miss ratio of the cache as a whole is the weighted average of the individual workload miss ratios, weighted by I/O rate:

$$m = \frac{1}{r} \sum_{i=1}^{n} r_i m_i \qquad (3.2)$$

We must now consider the error that results from replacing the correct miss ratio of each workload by the corresponding estimate $\hat{m}_i$, calculated using the average residency time of the cache as a whole. Using the proportionality relationship expressed by (1.19), the values $\hat{m}_i$ can be written as

$$\hat{m}_i = m_i \left(\frac{T}{T_i} \right)^{-\theta_i} \qquad (3.3)$$

Thus, the working hypothesis implies an overall miss ratio of

$$\hat{m} = \frac{1}{r} \sum_{i=1}^{n} r_i m_i \left(\frac{T}{T_i} \right)^{-\theta_i} \qquad (3.4)$$

To investigate the errors implied by this calculation, we write it in the alternative form

$$\hat{m} = \frac{1}{r} \sum_{i=1}^{n} r_i m_i \left[1 - (1 - \frac{T_i}{T})\right]^{\theta_i}$$

$$= \frac{1}{r} \sum_{i=1}^{n} r_i m_i (1 - \zeta_i)^{\theta_i}$$

were we define

$$\zeta_i = 1 - \frac{T_i}{T} \tag{3.5}$$

This expression for $\hat{m}$ can be expanded by applying the binomial theorem:

$$\hat{m} = \frac{1}{r} \sum_{i=1}^{n} r_i m_i [1 - \theta_i \zeta_i + \frac{1}{2}\theta_i(\theta_i - 1)\zeta_i^2 + o(\zeta_i^2)] \tag{3.6}$$

where the "little-o" notation indicates terms higher than second order.

Using (1.16), we define

$$\theta = 1 - \frac{\tau}{T}$$

to be the aggregate value of θ for the cache as a whole. Note, as a result, that in addition to the definition already given, ζ_i also has the equivalent definition

$$\zeta_i = 1 - \frac{1 - \theta}{1 - \theta_i} = \frac{\theta - \theta_i}{1 - \theta_i} \tag{3.7}$$

where we have applied (1.12) and taken advantage of the fact that each workload must share the same, common value of τ.

By applying (1.16)), we may rewrite the first-order terms of (3.6) as follows:

$$\frac{1}{r} \sum_{i=1}^{n} r_i m_i \theta_i \zeta_i = m \frac{1}{rm} \sum_{i=1}^{n} r_i m_i \theta_i (1 - \frac{T_i}{T})$$

$$= m \frac{1}{rm} \sum_{i=1}^{n} r_i m_i (1 - \frac{\tau}{T_i})(1 - \frac{T_i}{T})$$

$$= m \frac{1}{rm} \sum_{i=1}^{n} r_i m_i (1 - \frac{\tau}{T_i} - \frac{T_i}{T} + \frac{\tau}{T}) \tag{3.8}$$

But since each miss corresponds to a cache visit, the aggregate residency time is computed over misses; that is,

$$T = \frac{1}{rm} \sum_{i=1}^{n} r_i m_i T_i \tag{3.9}$$

so

$$\frac{1}{rm} \sum_{i=1}^{n} r_i m_i \frac{T_i}{T} = \frac{T}{T} = 1$$

and (3.8) reduces to

$$
\begin{aligned}
\frac{1}{r} \sum_{i=1}^{n} r_i m_i \theta_i \zeta_i &= \frac{\tau}{T} m - m \frac{1}{rm} \sum_{i=1}^{n} r_i m_i \frac{\tau}{T_i} \\
&= \frac{\tau}{T} m - \frac{\tau}{T} m \frac{1}{rm} \sum_{i=1}^{n} r_i m_i \frac{1}{1 - (1 - \frac{T_i}{T})} \\
&= \frac{\tau}{T} m - \frac{\tau}{T} m \frac{1}{rm} \sum_{i=1}^{n} r_i m_i (1 + (1 - \frac{T_i}{T}) + \zeta_i^2 + o(\zeta_i^2)) \\
&= \frac{\tau}{T} m - \frac{\tau}{T} m(2 - 1) + \frac{\tau}{T} m \frac{1}{rm} \sum_{i=1}^{n} r_i m_i (\zeta_i^2 + o(\zeta_i^2)) \\
&= (1 - \theta) m \frac{1}{rm} \sum_{i=1}^{n} r_i m_i (\zeta_i^2 + o(\zeta_i^2)) \qquad (3.10)
\end{aligned}
$$

Combining (3.2), (3.6), and (3.10), we now have

$$\hat{m} = m + m \frac{1}{rm} \sum_{i=1}^{n} r_i m_i \{[\theta - \frac{1}{2}\theta_i(1 - \theta_i) - 1]\zeta_i^2 + o(\zeta_i^2)\} \qquad (3.11)$$

Thus, $\hat{m} = m$ except for second-order and higher terms.

In a region sufficiently close to $\theta_1 = \theta_2 = \ldots = \theta_n = \theta$ (or equivalently, $T_1 = T_2 = \ldots = T_n = T$), the second-order and higher terms of (3.11) can be approximated as uniformly zero. The region where these second-order terms have at most a minor impact is that in which $|\zeta_i| \ll 1$ for $i = 1, 2, \ldots, n$. This requirement permits wide variations in the workloads sharing the cache.

For example, suppose that there are two workloads $i = 1, 2$, with values θ_i equal to .1 and .3 respectively; and suppose that these workloads share a cache in which, overall, we have $\theta = .2$. Then the absolute value of ζ_i is no greater than $.1/.7 = .14$ for either workload. As a result, the absolute value of either of the second order summation terms of (3.11), calculated without the summation weights $r_i m_i / rm$, does not exceed .02. But the summation of these terms, multiplied by the weights $r_i m_i / rm$, is merely a weighted average; so in the case of the example, the quantity just stated is the largest relative error, in either direction, that can be made by neglecting the second order terms (i.e. the error can be no larger than 2 percent of m). Since the second order terms are so relatively insignificant, we may conclude that the third-order and higher terms, shown as $o(\zeta_i^2)$, must be vanishingly small.

This chapter's working hypothesis has also proved itself in actual empirical use, without recourse to formal error analysis [22]. Its practical success confirms that the first-order approximation just obtained remains accurate within a wide enough range of conditions to make it an important practical tool.

Chapter 4

USE OF MEMORY AT THE I/O INTERFACE

In the traditional view of the memory hierarchy, the I/O interface forms a key boundary between levels. In this view, the level above the I/O interface consists of high speed processor memory; the level below consists of disk storage, which can store far more data, but requires physical movement, including disk rotation and head positioning, as part of data access.

The presence of storage control cache in modern storage controls has made for complications in the simple picture just described. Essentially similar semiconductor memory technologies now exist on *both* sides of the I/O interface. Since the the early 1980's, increasingly large file buffer areas, *and* increasingly large cache memories, have become available. This raises the question of how best to manage the deployment of semiconductor memory, some for file buffer areas and some for storage control cache, so as to maximize the gains in application performance.

The theme of this chapter is that, for most application data, it is possible to accomplish performance gains through a division of labor, in which each of the two memory technologies plays a specific role:

- File buffer areas, in the processor, are used to hold individual data records for long periods of time.

- Storage control cache contributes additional hits by staging the entire track of data following a requested record, and holding it for shorter times.

- In addition, storage control cache provides the capability to cache writes, which usually cannot be hardened in the processor buffers.

In broad terms, the objective of this strategy is to minimize the number of requests that must be serviced via physical disk access. Equivalently, the objective is to minimize the number of storage control cache misses. It is important to observe that this is *not* the same as wishing to maximize the number of storage control cache *hits*. Instead, we choose to service many or most application requests in the processor, without ever allowing them to appear as I/O operations. For this reason, the strategy just proposed may conflict with, and override, the frequently adopted objective of achieving high storage control hit ratios, measured as a percentage of I/O.

The initial two sections of the present chapter comprise a case study, in which we simulate the deployment of memory to support a range of specific files identified in one OS/390 trace. The final section uses the hierarchical reuse model to examine, in greater detail, the division of labor just proposed in the previous paragraph. We show that a balanced deployment of semiconductor memory, using both memory technologies, is likely to be the most cost-effective strategy for achieving high performance.

1.   SIMULATION USING TIME-IN-CACHE

To allow a detailed study of memory deployment, taking into account both processor memory and storage control cache, a simulation of both of these memory technologies and their interaction was developed. Some of the ideas previously introduced in Chapter 1, particularly the central concept of single-reference residency time, were applied to simplify the needed simulation software.

Misses in each type of memory were determined by applying the criterion of time-in-cache. So as to accomplish a division of labor between processor file buffers and storage control cache, a much longer single-reference residency time objective was adopted for the former than for the latter (600 seconds versus 60 seconds). Those I/O's identified as file buffer misses were placed into a side file, and became the input for a subsequent simulation of storage control cache. An additional storage control cache simulation was also performed based upon the original trace, so as to allow for the possibility that file buffering might not be present.

In all simulations, the cache memory requirements were calculated by accumulating, for each hit, the time since the requested data had been at the top of the LRU list. The average of such accumulated times yields a practical measurement of $g(\tau)$, whose theoretical definition is stated in (1.8). Based upon $g(\tau)$, the average residency time was computed by applying (1.9) and (1.7). Finally, the corresponding memory use was obtained from (1.18).

Note that this procedure is not subject to the sources of error examined in the previous chapter. If it is applied on a file-by-file basis, the procedure just described yields each file's individual cache residency time and memory requirements.

Moreover, it is possible to perform the analysis of any one file, independently of all other files. This fact was extremely helpful during the case study, since it meant that all memory deployment strategies of interest could be tested against all of the files. The most suitable deployment strategy for each file could then be selected afterward, based upon the simulation results.

2.   A CASE STUDY

We are now ready to apply the simulation, just discussed above, to a specific case study. The installation examined in the case study was a large OS/390 environment running primarily on-line database applications. More specifically, most applications were constructed using the Customer Information and Control System (CICS) to facilitate terminal interactions and manage database files. Databases constructed using DataBase 2 (DB2) and Information Management System (IMS) database management software were also in heavy use. Most database storage was contained in Virtual Storage Access Method (VSAM) files.

Our examination of the installation of the case study is based on a trace of all storage subsystem I/O during 30 minutes of the morning peak. The busiest 20 files (also called *data sets*) appearing in this trace are presented in Table 4.1. For each file, the table shows the processor and cache memory requirements needed to deliver single-reference residency times of 600 and 60 seconds, respectively. Also shown are the percentages of traced I/O requests that would be served out of processor or cache memory, given these memory sizes.

Note that the use of events traced at the I/O interface, as a base for the analysis presented in Table 4.1, represents a compromise. Conceptually, a more appealing alternative would be to base the analysis on a trace of the logical data requests made by the application, including those requests served in the processor without having to ask for data from disk. A key aim of the case study, however, was to capture a global picture of all disk activity, including all potential users of processor buffering or storage control cache. A global picture of this kind was believed to be practical only relative to events captured at the I/O interface.

Inasmuch as events at the I/O interface are the base for reporting, application requests that are hits in the existing processor buffers do not show up in the I/O trace and are not reflected in the projected percentages of I/O served by the processor. Only the additional I/O's that may be intercepted by adding more buffer storage are shown. The calculation of buffer memory requirements, as just described in the previous section, does, however, subsume the existing buffer storage (the simulated buffer storage must exceed the existing buffer storage before the simulation reports I/O's being handled as hits in the processor).

With the dynamic cache management facility of OS/390, it is possible to place "hints" into the I/O requests that access a given, selected file, recommending against the use of cache memory to store the corresponding data. Many controllers respond to such hints, either by not placing the data into cache memory,

Data Set	Memory Types Used		Processor Buffering Technique	I/O Rate	Projected Memory (MB)		Projected Percent of Trace I/O		
	CU?	PR?			Cache	Buffers	Disk Write	Served by Cache	Served by Buffers
IMS VSAM database	Y	Y	Hiperspace	58.0	2.8	8.7	0.9	2.6	96.1
CICS VSAM database	Y	Y	Hiperspace	26.6	1.0	13.2	0	3.2	95.4
DB2 index	Y	Y	Hiperpool	25.0	0.0	2.4	0.9	1.2	98.7
IMS VSAM database	Y	Y	Hiperspace	18.1	6.5	14.9	7.5	17.1	65.8
shared multi-db flat file	Y	N	n/a	16.2	23.4	0	2.1	33.2	0
JES2 checkpoint	Y	N	n/a	14.9	0.6	0	80.0	99.7	0
job scheduler flat file	Y	N	n/a	14.6	0.1	0	25.2	100	0
CICS load library	Y	Y	prog lib	13.6	1.0	21.5	1.1	2.8	93.1
JES2 spool storage	Y	N	n/a	13.6	3.3	0	66.9	91.6	0
JES2 spool storage	Y	N	n/a	13.3	3.3	0	68.5	91.8	0
SMF MAN1 flat file	Y	N	n/a	13.2	1.8	0	63.6	97.7	0
DB2 tablespace	Y	Y	Hiperpool	13.1	1.8	35.5	0.3	7.0	86.5
VVDS (catalog volume)	Y	N	n/a	12.8	0.0	0	0.1	100	0
JES2 spool storage	Y	N	n/a	12.7	3.3	0	69.3	91.1	0
JES2 spool storage	Y	N	n/a	11.7	3.1	0	68.1	90.9	0
DB2 tablespace	Y	Y	Hiperpool	11.5	2.9	27.0	0.4	13.1	75.0
CICS VSAM index	Y	Y	Hiperspace	11.5	0.0	0.0	0	0.0	99.9
DB2 tablespace	Y	Y	Hiperpool	10.7	1.2	14.1	0.3	8.9	86.6
CICS journal	Y	N	n/a	10.6	0.1	0	100	100	0
application work area	Y	N	n/a	10.2	0.6	0	100	98.9	0
Summaries for:									
			Hiperspace	730.9	377.7	467.7	16.3	43.0	38.0
			Hiperpool	192.0	46.2	327.8	10.2	22.1	66.4
			prog lib	89.2	10.6	61.8	3.6	25.8	69.4
			n/a	433.6	221.1	0	38.3	86.2	0

Table 4.1.   Busiest 20 files (data sets) in the case study.

or else by subjecting it to early demotion (this can be done by placing the data at or near the bottom of the LRU list when it is staged). Similarly, the system administrator can choose which databases should be supported by a given buffer pool. To take maximum advantage of this flexibility, the simulation results were placed into a spreadsheet, so that the option could be exercised, for each of the busiest installation files, whether or not to deploy that file's projected processor and storage control cache memory requirements. This choice is indicated by the two yes-or-no columns presented in Table 4.1.

Table 4.1 also indicates the method (if any) by which special, large buffer areas can be defined for use by a given file or group of files. More specifically, the figure refers to the following methods:

- Hiperspace: Special extensions of the VSAM Local Shared Resource buffer area.

- Hiperpool: Special DB2 buffer pool extensions.

- Prog lib: special storage for frequently used programs, provided through the Virtual Lookaside Facility/Library Lookaside (VLF/LLA).

The figure does not contain examples of the full range of facilities available for using large processor buffer areas in OS/390.

Some files, such as the CICS journal data set presented in Table 4.1, cannot make effective use of large processor buffer areas. For such files, Table 4.1 shows the deployment of storage control cache memory, but not the deployment of processor memory.

By contrast, a few small files exist (for example, certain program libraries) for which it is possible to obtain 100 percent hit ratios in the processor by setting aside enough buffer storage to contain them entirely. This can be done, however, for at most a very small fraction of all files, due to the immense ratio of disk relative to processor storage in a typical installation.

Since Table 4.1 shows the busiest 20 files observed during the case study, it should not be surprising that files required to perform system services (e.g. spool storage) play a prominent role. The table also, however, shows a number of examples of ordinary database files. It shows that such files, which typically represent the largest portion of installation storage, can make consistent, effective use of both processor storage and storage control cache.

For database files, the recommended amount of storage control cache, as shown in the table, is usually smaller than the amount of processor memory. This reflects the specialized role in which storage control cache has been deployed. Since storage control cache is used primarily to capture write operations, plus any read hits that come from staging an entire track of data rather than a single record, we project only a moderate amount of such cache as being necessary.

Because of their low percentages of read hits compared to overall reads, the databases presented by Table 4.1 might appear to be making ineffective use of storage control cache, if judged by the read-hit-ratio measure of cache effectiveness. Nevertheless, misses to these files, when applying the mixed strategy of memory use shown in the table, are substantially reduced compared with any other simulated strategy. The fact that this advantage is not reflected by the traditional read hit ratio metric suggests that too much prominence has been given to that metric in the traditional capacity planning process.

3.   EXPECTATIONS FOR MEMORY INTERACTION

As just shown in the previous section, objectives can be established for the single-reference residency time in storage control cache and in processor buffer areas, so that the two types of memory work cooperatively. But nevertheless, the functions provided by the two memories partially overlap. Read hits in the processor cannot also be hits in storage control cache. Does it really make sense to use both types of memory at the same time on the same data?

We now address this issue directly, using the hierarchical reuse model. Based upon this model, we shall demonstrate the following overall conclusions:

1. The best method of deploying a given memory budget is to use a relatively larger amount of processor storage, and a small to nearly equal amount of storage control cache.

2. Within this guideline, overall performance is highly insensitive to the exact ratio of memory sizes.

The second conclusion is extremely helpful in practical applications. For example, the analysis of the previous section takes advantage of it, by applying the same objectives for cache single reference residency time throughout Table 4.1. There is no need to fine-tune the objective specifically for those database files that also use large processor buffers; instead, it is merely necessary to adopt a residency time in the processor which exceeds that in the cache by a large margin. This yields a result that is sufficiently well balanced, given the second conclusion.

For simplicity in dealing with the fundamental issue of balancing the deployment of alternative memory technologies, we consider a reference pattern that consists of reads only. Also for simplicity, we assume a "plain vanilla" cache; thus, any reference to a track contained in the cache is considered to be a hit. The probability of a "front-end miss," normally very small, is assumed to be zero.

The equations (1.21) (for processor buffers) and (1.28) (for storage control cache) provide the key information needed for the analysis. These equations are sufficient to describe the miss ratios in both processor memory as well as storage control cache, as a function of the amount of memory deployed in each. The delay D to serve a given I/O request can therefore be estimated as well:

$$D = m_p D_p + m_p m'_c D_c \qquad (4.1)$$

where D_p is the increment of delay caused by a miss in processor memory (the time required to obtain data from storage control cache), and D_c is the additional increment of delay caused by a miss in the storage control cache (physical device service time less time for cache service).

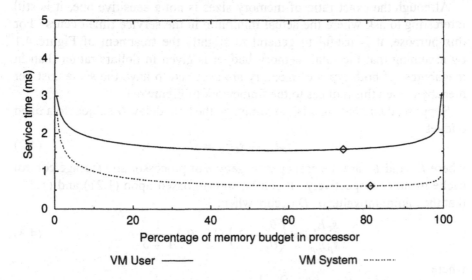

VM User ———   VM System ⋯⋯⋯

Figure 4.1. Tradeoff of memory above and below the I/O interface.

Figure 4.1 presents the result of applying (4.1) across the range of memory sizes that yield a fixed total size of one megabyte per I/O per second. This figure uses aggregate values for the VM user storage pools (solid line) and system storage pools (dashed line) initially presented in Figures 1.2 and 1.3. (For VM user storage pools, aggregate values of 0.25, 0.4, 0.125, and 0.7 were used for the parameters θ_c, a_c, θ_p, and a_p respectively; the aggregate parameter values used for VM system pools were 0.35, 0.35, 0.225, and 0.7 respectively). The quantities D_p and D_c are assumed to have the values 1.0 and 11.0 milliseconds, respectively (making total service time on the physical device equal to 12 milliseconds). For the extreme case where either memory size is zero, the miss ratio is taken to be unity. To avoid the lower limit of the hierarchical reuse time scale, the regions involving single-reference residency times of less than one second for either memory are bridged by interpolation.

The general form of Figure 4.1 confirms both of the assertions made at the beginning of the section. Among the allocation choices available within a fixed memory budget, the figure shows that a wide range of memory deployments are close to optimal. To hold service time delays to a minimum, the key is to adopt a balanced deployment, with a relatively larger amount of processor memory, and a small to nearly equal amount of storage control cache.

In the case study of the previous section, the deployment of memory was guided by adopting objectives for the corresponding single-reference residency times. The objective for processor memory was chosen to be ten times longer than that for storage control cache. Figure 4.1 shows the points where this factor-of-ten relationship holds for the user and system cases.

Although the exact ratio of memory sizes is not a sensitive one, it is still interesting to ask where the actual minimum in the service time occurs. For this purpose, it is useful to generalize slightly the treatment of Figure 4.1 by assuming that the total memory budget is given in dollars rather than in megabytes. If both types of memory are assumed to have the same cost per megabyte, then this reduces to the framework of Figure 4.1.

Suppose, then, that we wish to minimize the total delay D subject to a fixed budget

$$s_p E_p + s_c E_c = B \tag{4.2}$$

where E_p and E_c are the costs per megabyte of processor and storage control cache memory respectively. It can be shown, based upon (1.21) and (1.28), that the minimum value of D occurs when:

$$\frac{s_c E_c}{s_p E_p} = \left(\frac{\theta_c}{\theta_p} - 1\right)(1 - \theta_p)\frac{1}{1 + \delta} \tag{4.3}$$

where

$$\delta = \frac{D_p}{D_c}\frac{1}{m'_c}[1 - (\theta_c - \theta_p)]$$

Note, in applying (4.3), that it is necessary to iterate on the value of the cache miss ratio m'_c. The miss ratio must initially be set to an arbitrary value such as 0.5, then recomputed using (4.3), (1.21) and (1.28). Convergence is rapid, however; only three evaluations of (4.3) are enough to obtain a precise result.

In the present context, we are not so much interested in performing calculations based on (4.3) as in using it to gain insight. For this purpose, consider what happens if the goal is simply to minimize the number of requests served by the physical disks (this, in fact, is the broad description just given of our goal at the beginning of the present chapter). To accomplish that goal, we take into account only D_c, while assuming that D_p is zero. This simplification reduces (4.3) to

$$\frac{s_c E_c}{s_p E_p} = \left(\frac{\theta_c}{\theta_p} - 1\right)(1 - \theta_p) \tag{4.4}$$

Clearly, the crucial determinant of the best balance between the two memories, as specified by (4.4), is the difference in their *cache responsiveness* (i.e., values of θ). As long as there is any tendency for references to different individual records to cluster into groups, thereby causing a greater amount of use of a given track than of a given record, then some amount of storage control cache is appropriate. The stronger this tendency grows, the greater the role of storage control cache becomes in the optimum balance. Using as an example the values for θ of 0.25 in storage control cache and 0.125 in processor memory (the guestimates previously introduced in Chapter 1), (4.4) indicates that the fewest physical disk accesses occur when the ratio of the storage control and processor portions of the memory budget is

$$\left(\frac{0.25}{0.125} - 1\right)(1 - 0.125) = 0.875$$

This means that $1/(1+0.875) = 54$ percent of the total budget is allocated to the processor. If, instead, the values of θ are 0.35 in storage control cache and 0.225 in processor storage (typical values for the system data in Figure 4.1), we would allocate 70 percent of the total budget in the processor to get the fewest physical device accesses.

As indicated by (4.3), the memory balance that minimizes the total delay D involves a small upward adjustment in processor memory compared to the results just given. Assuming for simplicity that the cost of memory is the same in both the processor and the storage control, the fractions of the total storage needed in the processor to produce the minimal delay are 61 and 77 percent for the user and system cases, respectively.

It is worthwhile to reiterate that achieving the *optimum* balance is not important in practice. As Figure 4.1 shows, what matters is to achieve *some* balance, so that the larger portion of the memory budget is in the processor, and a small to nearly equal portion is in the storage control cache. This is sufficient to ensure that the delay per request is close to the minimum that can be achieved within the memory budget.

In a configuration that displays the desired balance of memories, the read hit ratio may well be below the sometimes recommended guideline of 70 percent. In the user and system configurations just discussed, that yield the minimum delay D, the storage control cache hit ratios are 67 and 73 percent, respectively. The potential for relatively low storage control hit ratios, in this configuration strategy, is mitigated by the overall load reduction due to processor buffering.

Chapter 5

MEMORY MANAGEMENT IN AN LRU CACHE

In previous chapters, we have argued that references to a given item of data tend to be transient. Thus, a sequence of requests to the data may "turn off" at any time; the most recently referenced items are the ones most likely to have remained the target of an ongoing request sequence. For data whose activity exhibits the behavior just described, the LRU algorithm seems to be a natural (if not even a compelling) choice for cache memory management. It provides what would appear to be the ideal combination of simplicity and effectiveness.

This chapter uses the multiple workload hierarchical reuse model to examine the performance of the LRU algorithm more closely. We focus particularly upon the special case $\theta_1 = \theta_2 = \cdots = \theta_n$, for two reasons:

1. The values of θ_i, for individual workloads within a given environment, often vary over a fairly narrow range.

2. In practical applications, a modeling approach based upon the special case $\theta_1 = \theta_2 = \cdots = \theta_n = \theta$ simplifies data gathering, since only an estimate of θ is needed.

In the special case $\theta_1 = \theta_2 = \cdots = \theta_n$, we find that the LRU algorithm is, in fact, optimal. As one reflection of this result, important in practical applications, we find that a memory partitioned by workload can perform as well as the same memory managed globally, only if the sizes of the partitions match with the allocations produced via global LRU management.

The final section of the chapter considers departures from the case $\theta_1 = \theta_2 = \cdots = \theta_n$. We find that we are able to propose a simple modification to the LRU algorithm, called Generalized LRU (GLRU) [23], that extends the optimality of the LRU scheme to the full range of conditions permitted by the multiple-workload hierarchical reuse model.

1.   THE CASE FOR LRU

In this section, our objective is to determine the best scheme for managing memory, given that the underlying data conforms to the multiple-workload hierarchical reuse model. For the present, we focus on the special case $\theta_1 = \theta_2 = \cdots = \theta_n$. In this special case, we shall discover that the scheme we are looking for is, in fact, the LRU algorithm.

As in Chapter 4, we consider the optimal use of memory to be the one that minimizes the total delay due to cache misses. We shall assume that a fixed delay $D_1 = D_2 = \cdots = D_n = D > 0$, measured in seconds, is associated with each cache miss. Also, we shall assume that all workloads share a common stage size $z_1 = z_2 = \cdots = z_n = z > 0$. We continue to assume, as in the remainder of the book, that the parameter θ lies in the range $0 < \theta < 1$. Finally, we shall assume that all workloads are non-trivial (that is, a non-zero I/O rate is associated with every workload). The final assumption is made without loss of generality, since clearly there is no need to allocate any cache memory to a workload for which no requests must be serviced.

We begin by observing that for any *individual* workload, data items have corresponding probabilities of being requested that are in descending order of the time since the previous request, due to (1.3). Therefore, for any *individual* workload, the effect of managing *that* workload's memory via the LRU mechanism is to place into cache memory exactly those data items which have the highest probabilities of being referenced next. This enormously simplifies our task, since we know how to optimally manage any given amount of memory assigned for use by workload i. We must still, however, determine the best trade-off of memory among the n workloads.

The optimal allocation of memory must be the one for which the marginal benefit (reduction of delays), per unit of added cache memory, is the same for all workloads. Otherwise, we could improve performance by taking memory away from the workload with the smallest marginal benefit and giving it to the workload with the largest benefit. At least in concept, it is not difficult to produce an allocation of memory with the same marginal benefit for all workloads, since, by the formula obtained in the immediately following paragraph, the marginal benefit for each workload is a strict monotonic decreasing function of its memory. We need only decide on some specific marginal benefit, and add (subtract) memory to (from) each workload until the marginal benefit reaches the adopted level. This same conceptual experiment also shows that there is a unique optimal allocation of memory corresponding to any given marginal benefit, and, by the same token, a unique optimal allocation corresponding to any given total amount of memory.

The next step, then, is to evaluate the marginal benefit of adding memory for use by any individual workload i. Using (1.23), we can write the delays due to misses, in units of seconds of delay per second of clock time, as:

$$D_i m_i r_i = D_i r_i b_i \left(\frac{s_i}{z_i b_i r_i}\right)^{-\frac{\theta_i}{1-\theta_i}}$$

$$= D_i r_i^{\frac{1}{1-\theta_i}} b_i \left(\frac{s_i}{z_i b_i}\right)^{-\frac{\theta_i}{1-\theta_i}} \tag{5.1}$$

Therefore, the marginal reduction of delays with added memory is:

$$-\frac{d(D_i m_i r_i)}{ds_i} = D_i \frac{\theta_i}{1-\theta_i} \frac{1}{z_i b_i} r_i^{\frac{1}{1-\theta_i}} b_i \left(\frac{s_i}{z_i b_i}\right)^{-\frac{\theta_i}{1-\theta_i}-1}$$

$$= \frac{D_i}{z_i} \frac{\theta_i}{1-\theta_i} \left(\frac{s_i}{z_i b_i r_i}\right)^{-\frac{1}{1-\theta_i}}$$

$$= \frac{D_i}{z_i T_i} \frac{\theta_i}{1-\theta_i}$$

by (1.21). Thus, we may conclude, by (1.12), that the marginal benefit of added memory is:

$$-\frac{d(D_i m_i r_i)}{ds_i} = \frac{\theta_i D_i}{z_i \tau_i} \tag{5.2}$$

But, for the purpose of the present discussion, we are assuming that all workloads share the same, common workload parameters θ, D, and z. To achieve optimal allocation, then, we must cause all of the workloads to share, as well, a common value $\tau_1 = \tau_2 = \cdots = \tau_n = \tau$ for the single-reference residency time. Only in this way can we have $\theta_1 D_1 / z_1 \tau_1 = \theta_2 D_2 / z_2 \tau_2 = \cdots = \theta_n D_n / z_n \tau_n = \theta D / z\tau$.

As we have seen, *exactly this behavior is accomplished by applying global LRU management*. A global LRU policy enforces LRU management of each individual workload's memory, while also causing all of the workloads to share the same, common single-reference residency time. For the special case $\theta_1 = \theta_2 = \cdots = \theta_n$, LRU management of cache memory is therefore optimal.

1.1   IMPACT OF MEMORY PARTITIONING

In the assumptions stated at the beginning of the section, we excluded those cases, such as a complete lack of I/O, in which any allocation of memory is as good as any other. Thus, we can also state the conclusion just presented as follows: a memory partitioned by workload can perform as well as the same memory managed globally, only if the sizes of the partitions match with the allocations produced via global LRU management.

Our ability to gain insight into the impact of subdivided cache memory is of some practical importance, since capacity planners must often examine the possibility of dividing a workload among multiple storage subsystems. In many cases there are compelling reasons for dividing a workload; for example, multiple subsystems may be needed to meet the total demand for storage, cache, and/or I/O throughput. But we have just seen that if such a strategy is implemented with no increase in total cache memory, compared with that provided with a single subsystem, then it may, as a side effect, cause some increase in the I/O delays due to cache misses. By extending the analysis developed so far, it is possible to develop a simple estimate of this impact, at least in the interesting special case in which a *single* workload is partitioned into n_p equal cache memories, and the I/O rate does not vary too much between partitions.

We begin by using (5.1) as a starting point. However, we now specialize our previous notation. A *single* workload, with locality characteristics described by the parameters b, θ, z, and D, is divided into n_p equal cache memories, each of size $s_p = s/n_p$. We shall assume that each partition $i = 1, 2, \ldots, n_p$ has a corresponding I/O rate r_i (that is, different partitions of the workload are assumed to vary only in their I/O rates, but not in their cache locality characteristics). These changes in notation result in the following, specialized version of (5.1):

$$Dm_i r_i = Dr_i^{\frac{1}{1-\theta}} b \left(\frac{s_p}{zb} \right)^{-\frac{\theta}{1-\theta}} \tag{5.3}$$

Our game plan will be to compare the total delays implied by (5.3) with the delays occurring in a global cache with the same total amount of memory $s = n_p s_p$. For the global cache, with I/O rate r, the miss ratio m is given by (1.23):

$$m = b \left(\frac{s}{zbr} \right)^{-\frac{\theta}{1-\theta}}$$

$$= b \left(\frac{s_p}{zb\bar{r}} \right)^{-\frac{\theta}{1-\theta}}$$

where $\bar{r} = r/n_p$ is the average I/O rate per partition. Therefore, we can express the corresponding total delays due to to misses, for the global cache, as

$$Dmr = Dn_p \bar{r} m = Dn_p \bar{r}^{\frac{1}{1-\theta}} b \left(\frac{s_p}{zb} \right)^{-\frac{\theta}{1-\theta}} \tag{5.4}$$

Turning again to the individual partitions, it is helpful to use the average partition I/O rate $\bar{r}$ as a point of reference. Thus, we normalize the individual partition I/O rates relative to $\bar{r}$:

$$r_i = \bar{r}(1 + \delta_i) \tag{5.5}$$

where

$$\delta_i = \frac{1}{\bar{r}}(r_i - \bar{r})$$

Our next step is to manipulate the right side of (5.5) by applying a binomial expansion. This technique places limits on the variations in partition I/O rates that we are able to take into account. At a minimum we must have $|\delta_i| < 1$ for $i = 1, 2, \ldots, n_p$ in order for the binomial expansion to be valid; for mathematical convenience, we shall also assume that the inequality is a strong one.

Provided, then, that the partition I/O rates do not vary by too much from their average value, we may apply the binomial theorem to obtain

$$r_i^{\frac{1}{1-\theta}} = \bar{r}^{\frac{1}{1-\theta}}[1 + \frac{1}{1-\theta}\delta_i + \frac{1}{2}\frac{1}{1-\theta}(\frac{1}{1-\theta} - 1)\delta_i^2 + \ldots]$$

$$\approx \bar{r}^{\frac{1}{1-\theta}}[1 + \frac{1}{1-\theta}\delta_i + \frac{1}{2}\frac{\theta}{(1-\theta)^2}\delta_i^2]$$

Using this expression to substitute into (5.3), the I/O delays due to misses in partition i are therefore given by:

$$Dm_i r_i \approx D\bar{r}^{\frac{1}{1-\theta}}b\left(\frac{s_p}{zb}\right)^{-\frac{\theta}{1-\theta}}[1 + \frac{1}{1-\theta}\delta_i + \frac{1}{2}\frac{\theta}{(1-\theta)^2}\delta_i^2]$$

$$= Dm\bar{r}[1 + \frac{1}{1-\theta}\delta_i + \frac{1}{2}\frac{\theta}{(1-\theta)^2}\delta_i^2]$$

where we have used (5.4) to obtain the second expression.

Taking the sum of these individual partition delays, we obtain a total of:

$$D\sum_{i=1}^{n_p} m_i r_i \approx Dn_p m\bar{r} + \frac{1}{1-\theta}Dm\bar{r}\sum_{i=1}^{n_p}\delta_i + \frac{1}{2}\frac{\theta}{(1-\theta)^2}Dm\bar{r}\sum_{i=1}^{n_p}\delta_i^2$$

But it is easily shown from the definition of the quantities δ_i that

$$\sum_{i=1}^{n_p}\delta_i = 0$$

and

$$\sum_{i=1}^{n_p}\delta_i^2 = \frac{n_p - 1}{\bar{r}^2}\text{Var}[r_i]$$

where Var[·] refers to the sample variance across partitions; that is,

$$\text{Var}[r_i] = \frac{1}{n_p - 1}\sum_{i=1}^{n_p}(r_i - \bar{r})^2$$

Therefore:

$$D \sum_{i=1}^{n_p} m_i r_i \approx Drm + \frac{1}{2} Drm \frac{n_p - 1}{n_p} \frac{\theta}{(1 - \theta)^2} \frac{\text{Var}[r_i]}{\bar{r}^2}$$

Since the term involving the sample variance is always non-negative, the total delay can never be less than Drm (the total delay of the global cache). If we now let

$$m_p = \frac{1}{r} \sum_{i=1}^{n_p} m_i r_i$$

be the weighted average miss ratio of the partitioned cache, weighted by I/O rate, then we can restate our conclusion in terms of the average delay per I/O:

$$m_p D = (1 + \epsilon) m D \qquad (5.6)$$

where ϵ, the relative "penalty" due to partitioning, is given by:

$$\epsilon \approx \frac{1}{2} \frac{n_p - 1}{n_p} \frac{\theta}{(1 - \theta)^2} \frac{\text{Var}[r_i]}{\bar{r}^2}$$

In applying (5.6), it should be noted that the value of ϵ is not affected if all the I/O rates are scaled using a multiplicative constant. Thus, we may choose to express the partition I/O rates as events per second, as fractions of the total load, or even as fractions of the largest load among the n_p partitions.

A "rule of thumb" that is sometimes suggested is that, on average, two storage subsystems tend to divide the total I/O rate that they share in a ratio of 60 percent on one controller, 40 percent on the other. This guestimate provides an interesting illustration of (5.6).

Suppose that both subsystems, in the rule of thumb, have the same amount of cache memory and the same workload characteristics. Let us apply (5.6) to assess the potential improvement in cache performance that might come from consolidating them into a single subsystem with double the amount of cache memory possessed by either separately. Since we do not know the actual I/O rates, and recalling that we may work in terms of fractions of the total load, we proceed by setting r_1 and r_2 to values of .4 and .6 respectively. The sample variance of these two quantities is $(.1^2 + .1^2)/(2 - 1) = .02$. Assuming $\theta = 0.25$, we thus obtain $\epsilon \approx \frac{1}{2} \times \frac{1}{2} \times (.25/.75^2) \times (.02/.5^2) \approx .009$.

Based upon the calculation just presented, we conclude that the improvement in cache performance from consolidating the two controllers would be very slight (the delay per I/O due to cache misses would be reduced by less than one percent). From a practical standpoint, this means that the decision on whether to pursue consolidation should be based on other considerations, not dealt with in the present analysis. Such considerations would include, for example, the cost of the combined controller, and its ability to deliver the needed storage and I/O throughput.

2.   GENERALIZED LRU

Within our adopted analysis framework, we have seen that the LRU algorithm is optimal in the case that $\theta_1 = \theta_2 = \cdots = \theta_n$. We now show that it is also possible to extend the LRU algorithm, so as to achieve optimality under the full range of conditions permitted by the multiple-workload hierarchical reuse model.

As before, our starting point is the marginal benefit of cache memory. Our objective is to arrange matters so that the marginal benefit, as stated by (5.2), is the same for all workloads i. To accomplish this, we now observe that *the quantity (5.2) is the same for all i if and only if τ_i is proportional to $\theta_i D_i / z_i$*. To accomplish an optimal arrangement of cache memory, we may therefore proceed by adjusting the single reference residency times of the individual workloads, so as to achieve the proportionality relationship just stated.

It should be recalled that the value of θ_i, for a given workload, can be estimated from measurements of τ_i and T_i (this relationship is stated by (1.16)). By associating cached data with timestamps showing the time of the most recent reference, it is not difficult, in turn, to measure the quantities T_i and τ_i. To measure τ_i, for example, one approach is to occasionally place *dummy entries* (entries with no associated data) into the LRU list alongside the entries being staged for workload i. When a dummy entry reaches the bottom of the LRU list, the time since it was initially placed into the list provides a direct measurement of the single-reference residency time. Similarly, the discussion of simulation techniques, previously presented in Chapter 4, includes a method for using cache entry timestamps to measure the quantities T_i.

To establish the desired proportionality relationship, our first step is to associate each cached item of data with a timestamp showing the time of last reference, and to use these timestamps as a basis for measuring the quantities T_i, τ_i, and θ_i. Optionally, we may also choose to assign workload-specific values to the quantities z_i and D_i, or we may choose to assume, as in the previous section, that these quantities do not vary between workloads.

Among the workloads, let workload k be one for which $\theta_k D_k / z_k \geq \theta_i D_i / z_i$, $1 \leq i \leq n$ (if there is more than one such workload, break the tie at random). We may now generalize the LRU algorithm as follows:

1. When inserting data items associated with workload k into the LRU list, as the result of either a stage or a hit, place them at the top.

2. When inserting data items associated with other workloads $i \neq k$ into the LRU list, as the result of either a stage or a hit, place them at insertion points such that

$$\frac{\tau_i}{\tau_k} \approx \frac{\theta_i D_i z_k}{\theta_k D_k z_i} \tag{5.7}$$

In (5.7), the inequality reflects the measurement and other errors that must be expected in any practical implementation. In an idealized, error-free implementation, (5.7) would instead specify equality.

A technique by which to accomplish step (2), with minimal linked-list "housekeeping", is to apply, once more, the concept of dummy entries. This time, the dummy entries act as insertion points. Periodically (for example, every 10 seconds), a new insertion point of this type is placed at the top of the LRU list. At the same time, a pointer to it is placed at the tail of a circular queue. When the insertion point ages out (reaches the bottom of the LRU list), the pointer is removed from the head of the queue. Let n_Q be the number of entries currently on the queue, and let the positions $0 \leq Q \leq n_Q - 1$ of these entries be counted, starting from position 0 at the head, up to position $n_Q - 1$ at the tail. Since the placement of insertion points at the top of the LRU list is scheduled at regular intervals, the remaining time for data at the associated list positions to age out must increase in approximately equal steps, as we move from the head to the tail of the circular queue. As the insertion point for workload i, we may therefore choose the one found at the circular queue position $Q_i = \lceil (n_Q - 1) \times \tau_i / \tau_k \rceil$, where the ratio τ_i / τ_k is specified based upon (5.7).

Taking a step back, and recalling (1.16), it should be emphasized that the proposed algorithm is, by design, sensitive to workload characteristics that contribute to *front-end* time, as previously discussed in Chapter 1. Thus, we allocate larger amounts of memory to workloads that exhibit longer times between hits. By contrast, we allocate relatively little memory to workloads where bursts of hits occur in rapid succession. From this standpoint, the GLRU algorithm can be viewed as a way of extending the key insight reflected, in many controllers, by their placement of sequential data at the bottom of the LRU list.

The GLRU algorithm, as just proposed, is one of many improvements to the LRU algorithm that various authors have suggested [9, 24, 25, 26]. Within the analysis framework which we have adopted, however, an exact implementation of the GLRU algorithm (one that accomplishes equality in (5.7)) produces the unique, optimum allocation of cache memory: that at which the marginal benefit of more cache is the same for all workloads.

Most other proposals for extending the LRU algorithm provide some mechanism by which to shape the management of a given data item by observing its pattern of activity. For example, in the LRU-K algorithm, the data item selected for replacement is the one that possesses the least recent reference, taking into account the last K references to each data item. As a result, this scheme selects the data item with the slowest average rate of activity, based upon the period covered by the last K references and extending up to the present time.

The GLRU algorithm, by contrast, determines the insertion point of a given data item when it is staged, and this insertion point is unlikely to undergo significant evolution or adjustment during any single cache visit. This reflects our overall perspective that the activity of a given item of data is, in general, too transient for observations of its behavior to pay off while it is still in cache. The GLRU algorithm does observe ongoing patterns of reference, but the objective of such observations is to make available more information about the *workload*, so as to improve the insertion point used for data still to be staged.

It should be apparent that the property of optimality depends strongly upon the framework of analysis. An interesting alternative framework, to the probabilistic scheme of the present section, is that in which the the strategy of cache management is based upon the entire sequence of requests (that is, the decision on what action to take at a given time incorporates knowledge of subsequent I/O requests). Within that framework, it has been shown that the best cache entry to select for replacement is the one that will remain unreferenced for the longest time [27]. This scheme results in what is sometimes called the Longest Forward Reference (LFR) algorithm. Some conceptual tie would seem to exist between the LFR and GLRU algorithms, in that, although the GLRU algorithm does not assume detailed knowledge of future events, it *does*, prior to a given cache visit, make statistical inferences about the cache visits that should be expected for a given workload.

The independent reference model, previously introduced in Chapter 1, has also been used as an analysis framework within which it is possible to identify an optimum memory management algorithm. Within that framework, it has been shown that the LRU-K algorithm is optimal, among those algorithms that use information about the times of the most recent K or fewer references [9]. As previously discussed in Chapter 1, however, the independent reference model is not well-suited to the description of the transient patterns of access typical of most memory hierarchies.

Finally, it should again be repeated that the LRU algorithm, with no generalizations at all, offers an outstanding combination of simplicity and effectiveness.

Chapter 6

FREE SPACE COLLECTION IN A LOG

The log-structured disk subsystem is still a relatively new concept for the use of disk storage. First proposed by Ousterhout and Douglis in 1989 [28], practical systems of this type have gained widespread acceptance in the disk storage marketplace since the mid-1990's. When implemented using disk array technology [29], such systems are also called *Log Structured Arrays* (LSA's).

In the log-structured scheme for laying out disk storage, all writes are organized into a log, each entry of which is placed into the next available free area on disk. A directory indicates the physical location of each logical data item (e.g., each file block or track image). For those data items that have been written more than once, the directory retains the location of the most recent copy.

The log-based approach to handling writes offers the important advantage that, when a data item is updated, storage is re-allocated for it so that it can be placed at the head of the log. This contrasts with the more traditional approach, in which storage for the data item is recycled by overwriting one copy with another. Due to storage re-allocation, the new copy can occupy any required amount of space; the new and old copies need not be identical in size as would be required for updating in place. This flexibility allows the log-structured scheme to accommodate the use of compression technology much more easily than would be possible with the traditional update-in-place approach.

The flip side of storage re-allocation, however, is that data items that have been rendered out-of-date accumulate. Over time, the older areas of the log become fragmented due to storage occupied by such items. A de-fragmenting process (*free space collection*, also called *garbage collection*), is needed to consolidate still-valid data and to recycle free storage.

Understanding the requirements of the free space collection process is among the new challenges posed by log-structured disk technology. Such understanding is required both to assess the impact of free space collection on device performance, as well as to correct performance problems in cases where free space collection load is excessive. In many studies, the demands for free space collection have been investigated via trace-driven simulation [28, 30, 31].

The present chapter investigates *analytically* the amount of data movement that must be performed by the free space collection process. By taking advantage of the hierarchical reuse model, we develop a realistic analysis of the relationship between free space collection and the storage utilization of the disk subsystem. Thus, the hierarchical reuse model yields an assessment of the degree to which we can reasonably expect to fill up physical disk storage.

When examining free space collection loads, the focus is on the disk storage medium; other aspects of storage subsystem operation, such as cache memory, play the role of peripheral concerns. For this reason, we shall adopt the convention, within the present chapter *only*, that the term *write* refers to an operation at the physical disk level. Thus, within the present chapter, the phrase *data item write* is a shorthand way of referring to the operation of copying the data item from cache to disk (also called a *cache destage*), after the item was previously written by the host.

The methods of analysis developed in this chapter assume that no spare free space is held in reserve. This assumption is made without loss of generality, since to analyze a subsystem with spare storage held in reserve we need only limit the analysis to the subset of storage that is actually in use. Note, however, that in a practical log-structured subsystem, at least a small buffer of spare free space must be maintained.

The practical applicability of the results of the present chapter is greatly enhanced by the fact that they are *very* easy to summarize. The following paragraphs provide a sketch of the central results.

The initial two sections of the chapter provide an overall description of the free space collection process, and a "first cut" at the problem of free space collection performance. The "first cut" approach, which is chosen for its simplicity rather than its realism, yields the result:

$$M = \frac{.5}{1 - u} - 1 \tag{6.1}$$

where u is the storage utilization (fraction of physical storage occupied) and M is the average number of times a given data item must be moved during its lifetime. Since the life of each data item ends with a write operation that causes the item's log entry to be superseded, the metric M is also called *moves per write*.

To interpret (6.1), it is helpful to choose some specific example for the storage utilization (say, 75 percent). In the case of this specific storage utilization, (6.1) says that, for each data item written by the host, an average of one data item must be moved (i.e. read from one location and written back to another). For storage utilizations higher than 75 percent, the number of moves per write increases rapidly, and becomes unbounded as the utilization approaches 100 percent.

The most important implication of (6.1) is that the utilization of storage should not be pushed much above the range of 80 to 85 percent full, less any storage that must be set aside as a free space buffer. To put this in perspective, it should be noted that *traditional* disk subsystems must *also* be managed so as to provide substantial amounts of free storage. Otherwise, it would not be practical to allocate new files, and increase the size of old ones, on an as-needed basis. The amount of free space needed to ensure moderate freespace collection loads tends to be no more than that set aside in the case of traditional disk storage management [32].

The final two sections of the chapter show, in a nutshell, that (6.1) continues to stand up as a reasonable "rule of thumb", even after accounting for a much more realistic model of the free space collection process than that initially presented to justify the equation. This is because, to improve the realism of the model, we we must take into account two effects:

1. the impact of transient patterns of data reference within the workload, and

2. the impact of algorithm improvements geared toward the presence of such patterns.

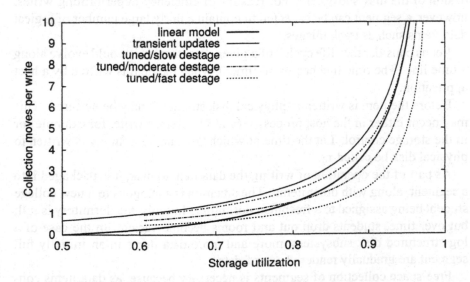

Figure 6.1. Overview of free space collection results.

One section is devoted to each of these effects. As we shall show, effects (1) and (2) work in opposite directions, insofar as their impact on the key metric M is concerned. A reasonable objective, for the algorithm improvements of (2), is to ensure a level of free space collection efficiency at least as good as that stated by (6.1).

Figure 6.1 illustrates impacts (1) and (2), and provides, in effect, a road map for the chapter. The heavy solid curve (labeled *linear model*), presents the "rule-of-thumb" result stated by (6.1). The light solid curve (labeled *transient updates*), presents impact (1). The three dashed lines (labeled *tuned / slow destage*, *tuned / moderate destage*, and *tuned / fast destage*) present three cases of impact (2), which are distinguished from each other by how rapidly writes performed at the application level are written to the disk medium.

1.   THE LIFE CYCLE OF LOGGED DATA

In a log-structured disk subsystem, the "log" is not contiguous. Succeeding log entries are written into the next available storage, wherever it is located. Obviously, however, it would be impractical to allocate and write the log one byte at a time. To ensure reasonable efficiency, it is necessary to divide the log into physically contiguous *segments*. A *segment*, then, is the unit into which writes to the log are grouped, and is the smallest usable area of free space. By contrast with the sizes of data items, which may vary, the size of a segment is fixed. The disk storage in a segment is physically contiguous, and may also conform to additional requirements in terms of physical layout.

A segment may contain various amounts of data, depending upon the detailed design of the disk subsystem. For reasons of efficiency in performing writes, however, a segment can be expected to contain a fairly large number of logical data items such as track images.

Let us consider the "life cycle" of a given data item, as it would evolve along a time line. The time line begins, at time 0, when the item is written by a host application.

Before the item is written to physical disk storage, it may be buffered. This may occur either in the host processor (a DB2 deferred write, for example) or in the storage control. Let the time at which the data item finally is written to physical disk be called τ_0.

As part of the operation of writing the data item to disk, it is packaged into a segment, along with other items. The situation is analogous to a new college student being assigned to a freshman dormitory. Initially, the dormitory is full; but over time, students drop out and rooms become vacant. In the case of a log structured disk subsystem, more and more data items in an initially full segment are gradually rendered out-of-date.

Free space collection of segments is necessary because, as data items contained in them are superseded, unused storage builds up. To recycle the unused storage, the data that are still valid must be copied out so that the segment becomes available for re-use — just as, at the end of the year, all the freshmen who are still left move out to make room for next year's class.

In the above analogy, we can imagine setting aside different dormitories for different ages of students — e.g., for freshmen, sophomores, juniors and seniors. In the case of dormitories, this might be for social interaction or mutual aid in studying. There are also advantages to adopting a similar strategy in a log-structured disk subsystem. Such a strategy creates the option of administering various segments differently, depending upon the age of the data contained in them.

To simplify the present analysis as much as possible, we shall assume that the analogy sketched above is an exact one. Just as there might be a separate set of dormitories for each year of the student population, we shall assume that there is one set of segments for storing brand new data; another set of segments for storing data that have been copied exactly once; another for data copied twice; and so forth.

Moreover, since a given segment contains a large number of data items, segments containing data of a given age should take approximately the same length of time to incur any given number of invalidations. For this reason, we shall assume that segments used to store data that have been copied exactly once consistently retain such data for about the same amount of time before it is collected, and similarly for segments used to store data that have been copied exactly twice, exactly three times, and so forth.

To describe how this looks from the viewpoint of a given data item, it is helpful to talk in terms of *generations*. Initially, a data item belongs to generation 1 and has never been copied. If it lasts long enough, the data item is copied and thereby enters generation 2; is copied again and enters generation 3; and so forth. We shall use the constants $\tau_1, \tau_2, \ldots$, to represent the times (as measured along each data item's own time line) of the move operations just described. That is, $\tau_i, i = 1, 2, \ldots$, represents the age of a given data item when it is copied out of generation i.

2.   FIRST-CUT PERFORMANCE ESTIMATE

Let us now consider the amount of data movement that we should expect to occur, within the storage management framework just described.

If all of the data items in a segment are updated at the same time, then the affected segment does not require free space collection, since no valid data remains to copy out of it. An environment with mainly sequential files should tend to operate in this way. The performance implications of free space collection in a predominately sequential environment should therefore be minimal.

In the remainder of this chapter, we focus on the more scattered update patterns typical of a database environment. To assess the impact of free space collection in such an environment, two key parameters must be examined: the moves per write M, and the utilization of storage u. Both parameters are driven by how empty a segment is allowed to become before it is collected. Let us assume that segments are collected, in generation i, when their storage utilization falls to the threshold value f_i.

A key further decision which we must now make is whether the value of the threshold f_i should depend upon the generation of data stored in the segment. If $f_1 = f_2 = \cdots. = f$, then the collection policy is *history independent* since the age of data is ignored in deciding which segments to collect. It may, however, be advantageous to design a *history dependent* collection policy in which different thresholds are applied to different generations of data. The possibilities offered by adopting a history dependent collection policy are examined further in the final section of the chapter. In the present section, we shall treat the collection threshold as being the same for all generations.

Given, then, a fixed collection threshold f, consider first its effect on the moves per write M. The fraction of data items in any generation that survive to the following generation is given by f, since this is the fraction of data items that are moved when collecting the segment. Therefore, we can enumerate the following possible outcomes for the life cycle of a given data item:

- The item is never moved before being invalidated (probability $1 - f$).

- The item is moved exactly once before being invalidated (probability $f \times (1 - f)$).

- The item is moved exactly $i = 2, 3, \ldots$ times before being invalidated (probability $f^i \times (1 - f)$).

These probabilities show that the number of times that a given item is moved conform to a well-known probability distribution, i.e. the *geometric* distribution with parameter f. The average number of moves per write, then, is given by the average value of the geometric distribution:

$$M = \frac{f}{1 - f} \tag{6.2}$$

Note that the moves per write become unbounded as f approaches unity.

Next, we must examine the effect of the free space collection policy on the subsystem storage utilization u. Intuitively, it is clear that to achieve high storage utilization, a high value of f will be required so as to minimize the amount of unused storage that can remain uncollected in a segment.

There is a specific characteristic of the pattern of update activity which, if it applies, simplifies the analysis enormously. This characteristic involves the average utilization experienced by a given segment over its lifetime (the period between when the segment is first written to disk and when it is collected). If this average utilization depends upon the collection threshold f in the same way, regardless of the generation of the data in the segment, then we shall say that the workload possesses a *homogeneous* pattern of updates. Both the simple model of updates that we shall assume in the present section, as well as the hierarchical reuse model examined in the following section, exhibit homogeneous updates.

If the pattern of updates is homogeneous, then all segments that are collected based on a given threshold will have the same average utilization over their lifetimes. In the case of a single collection threshold for all segments, a single lifetime utilization must also apply. This utilization must therefore also be the average utilization of the subsystem as a whole, assuming that all segments are active.

Let us now make what is undoubtedly the simplest possible assumption about the pattern of updates during the life of a segment: that the rate of rendering data objects invalid is a constant. In the dormitory analogy, this assumption would say that students drop out at the same rate throughout the school year. We shall call this assumption the *linear model* of free space collection.

By the linear model, the utilization of a given segment must decline, at a constant rate, from unity down to the value of the collection threshold. Therefore the average storage utilization over the life of the segment is just:

$$u = \frac{1+f}{2} \qquad (6.3)$$

Since this result does not depend upon generation, the linear model has a homogeneous pattern of updates. Equation (6.3) gives the average lifetime utilization for any segment, regardless of generation. Therefore, (6.3) also gives the utilization of the subsystem as a whole, assuming that all segments are active (i.e., assuming that no free space is held in reserve). As expected, storage utilization increases with f.

We need now merely use (6.3) to substitute for f in (6.2). This yields the result previously stated as (6.1):

$$M = \frac{.5}{1-u} - 1$$

This result is shown as the heavy solid curve in Figure 6.1. It shows clearly that as the subsystem approaches 100 percent full, the free space collection load becomes unbounded. This conclusion continues to stand up as we refine our results to obtain the remaining curves presented in the figure.

It should be noted that, due to our assumption that all segments are active, (6.1) applies only to storage utilizations of at least 50 percent. For lower utilizations, the linear model can apply *only* if some segments are held in reserve. By (6.3), there is no other way to achieve an average segment utilization outside the range of 50–100 percent.

3.   IMPACT OF TRANSIENT DATA ACCESS

Returning to the dormitory analogy, we have just assumed, in the preceding analysis, that students drop out at a constant rate. This assumption is not very realistic, however. We should more correctly anticipate a larger number of students to drop out in the first term than in subsequent terms. Similarly, once a fresh data item is written into a segment, we should expect, due to transient data access, that the probability of further updates is highest shortly afterward.

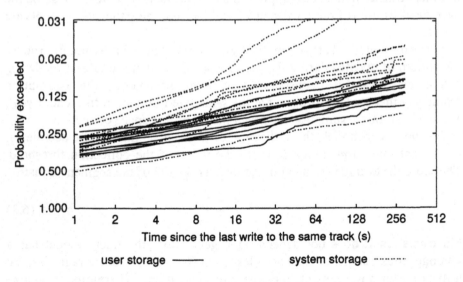

Figure 6.2.   Distribution of time between track updates, for the user and system storage pools also presented in Figure 1.2.

The hierarchical reuse model provides the ideal mathematical device with which to examine this effect. To do so, we need merely proceed by assuming that (1.3) applies, not only to successive data item references in general, but also to successive *writes*. Figure 6.2 helps to justify this assumption. It presents the distribution of interarrival times between writes, for the same VM user and system storage pools that we first examined in Chapter 1. Note, in comparing Figure 6.2 (writes) with Figure 1.2 (all references), that a small difference in slopes is apparent (say, $\theta \approx 0.2$ for writes as contrasted with $\theta \approx 0.25$ for all references).

Despite Figure 6.2, the application of the hierarchical reuse model to free space collection does represent something of a "leap of faith". The time scales relevant to free space collection are much longer than those presented in Figure

6.2. The appropriate time scales would extend from a few minutes, up to several days or weeks.

Nevertheless, the hierarchical reuse model greatly improves the realism of our previous analysis. We need no longer assume that data items are rendered invalid at a constant rate. Instead, the rate of invalidation starts at some initial level, then gradually tails off.

Since an aging segment spends varying amounts of time in each state of occupancy, it is necessary to apply Little's law to calculate the *average* utilization of a given segment, during its lifetime. Let w_i be the average rate at which new data items are added to generation i (also, note that $w_1 = w$, the rate of new writes into storage as a whole). Let $F(\cdot)$ be the cumulative distribution of the lifetime of a data item, and define

$$T_i = \frac{\int_{\tau_{i-1}}^{\tau_i} x \, dF(x)}{F(\tau_i) - F(\tau_{i-1})} \tag{6.4}$$

to be the average lifetime of those data items that become out of date during the life of the segment. Consider, now, the collection of segments that provide storage for generation i, $i = 1, 2, \ldots$.

On the one hand, the total number of data item's worth of storage in the segments of generation i, counting the storage of both valid and invalid data items, must be:

$$w_i(\tau_i - \tau_{i-1})$$

by Little's law. On the other hand, the population of data items that are still valid is

$$w_i\{f_i(\tau_i - \tau_{i-1}) + (1 - f_i)(T_i - \tau_{i-1})\}$$

since a fraction $1 - f_i$ of the items are rendered invalid before being collected. We can therefore divide storage in use by total storage, to obtain:

$$u_i = f_i + \frac{T_i - \tau_{i-1}}{\tau_i - \tau_{i-1}}(1 - f_i) \tag{6.5}$$

Recalling that (6.5) applies regardless of the distribution of data item lifetimes, we must now specialize this result based upon the hierarchical reuse model. In this special case, the following interesting relationship results from the definition of f_i:

$$f_i = \frac{1 - F(\tau_i)}{1 - F(\tau_{i-1})}$$

$$= \left(\frac{\tau_i}{\tau_{i-1}}\right)^{-\theta} \tag{6.6}$$

To specialize (6.5), we must successively plug (1.10) into (6.4), then the result into (6.5). A full account of these calculations is omitted due to length. Eventually, however, they yield the simple and interesting result:

$$u_i = \frac{1}{1-\theta} \frac{f_i - f_i^{1/\theta}}{1 - f_i^{1/\theta}} \tag{6.7}$$

The average segment utilization, as shown in (6.7), depends upon f_i in the same way, regardless of the specific generation i. Therefore, *the hierarchical reuse model exhibits a homogeneous pattern of updates.*

Consider, then, the case $f_1 = f_2 = \cdots = f$. In a similar manner to the results of the previous section, (6.7) gives, not only the average utilization of segments belonging to each generation i, but also the average utilization of storage as a whole:

$$u = \frac{1}{1-\theta} \frac{f - f^{1/\theta}}{1 - f^{1/\theta}} \tag{6.8}$$

The two equations (6.2) and (6.8), taken together, determine M as a function of u, since they specify how these two quantities respectively are driven by the collection threshold. The light, solid curve of Figure 6.1 presents the resulting relationship, assuming the guestimate $\theta \approx 0.20$.

As shown by the figure, the net impact of transient data access is to increase the moves per write that are needed at any given storage utilization. Keeping in mind that both of these quantities are driven by the collection threshold, the reason for the difference in model projections is that, at any given collection threshold, the utilization projected by the hierarchical reuse model is lower than that of the linear model.

To examine more closely the relationship between the two projected utilizations, it is helpful to write the second-order expansion of (6.8) in the neighborhood of $f = 1$:

$$\begin{aligned} u &\approx 1 - \frac{1-f}{2} - \frac{1+\theta}{12\theta}(1-f)^2 \\ &= \frac{1+f}{2} - \frac{1+\theta}{12\theta}(1-f)^2 \end{aligned} \tag{6.9}$$

This gives a practical approximation for values of f greater than about 0.6. As a comparison of (6.3) and (6.9) suggests, the utilization predicted by the hierarchical reuse model is always less than that given by the linear model, but the two predictions come into increasingly close agreement as the collection threshold approaches unity.

4.   HISTORY DEPENDENT COLLECTION

As we have just found, the presence of transient patterns of update activity has the potential to cause a degradation in performance. Such transient patterns also create an opportunity to improve performance, however. This can be done by delaying the collection of a segment that contains recently written data items, until the segment is mostly empty. As a result, it is possible to avoid ever moving a large number of the data items in the segment.

Such a delay can only be practical if it is limited to recently written data; segments containing older data would take too long to empty because of the slowing rate of invalidation. Therefore, a history dependent free space collection strategy is needed to implement this idea. In this section, we investigate what would appear to be the simplest history dependent scheme: that in which the collection threshold f_1, for generation 1, is reduced compared to the common threshold f_h that is shared by all other generations.

To obtain the moves per write in the history dependent case, we must add up two contributions:

1. Moves from generation 1 to generation 2. Such moves occur at a rate of wf_1.

2. Moves among generations 2 and higher. Once a data item reaches generation 2, the number of additional moves can be obtained by the same reasoning as that applied previously in the history independent case: it is given as the mean of a geometric distribution with parameter f_h. Taking into account the rate at which data items reach generation 2, this means that the total rate of moves, among generations 2 and higher, is given by:

$$wf_1 \frac{f_h}{1 - f_h}$$

If we now add both contributions, this means that:

$$
\begin{aligned}
M &= \frac{1}{w} \times wf_1[1 + \frac{f_h}{1 - f_h}] \\
&= \frac{f_1}{1 - f_h}
\end{aligned}
\tag{6.10}
$$

Just we analyzed history independent storage in the previous section, we must now determine the storage utilization that should be expected in the history dependent case. Once more, we proceed by applying Little's law.

Let s be total number of data items the subsystem has the physical capacity to store, broken down into generation 1 (denoted by s_1) and generations 2, 3, ... (denoted collectively by s_h). Likewise, let u be total subsystem storage utilization, broken down into u_1 and u_h. Then by Little's law, we must have $Tw = us$, where T is the average lifetime of a data item before invalidation.

It is important to note, in this application of Little's law, that the term "average lifetime" must be defined carefully. For the purpose of understanding a broad range of system behavior, it is possible to define the average time spent in a system based upon events that occur during a specific, finite period of time [33]. In the present analysis, a long, but still finite, time period would be appropriate (for example, one year). This approach is called the *operational* approach to performance evaluation. Moreover, *Little's law remains valid when the average time spent in a system is defined using the conventions of operational analysis.* In the definition of T, as just stated in the previous paragraph, we now add the caveat that "average lifetime" must be interpreted according to operational conventions. This caveat is necessary to ensure that T is well defined, even in the case that the standard statistical expectation of T, as computed by applying (1.3), may be unbounded.

Keeping Little's law in mind, let us now examine the components of us:

$$\begin{aligned} Tw &= us \\ &= u_1 s_1 + u_h s_h \\ &= u_1 w(\tau_1 - \tau_0) + u_h s_h \\ &= (u_1 - u_h)w(\tau_1 - \tau_0) + u_h[w(\tau_1 - \tau_0) + s_h] \\ &= (u_1 - u_h)w(\tau_1 - \tau_0) + u_h s \end{aligned}$$

Thus,

$$s = \frac{Tw}{u_h} + (1 - \frac{u_1}{u_h})w(\tau_1 - \tau_0)$$

Since, as just noted, $s = Tw/u$, this means that:

$$\frac{1}{u} = \frac{1}{u_h} + (1 - \frac{u_1}{u_h})\left(\frac{\tau_1}{T} - \frac{\tau_0}{T}\right) \tag{6.11}$$

Finally, we must specialize this result, which applies regardless of the specific workload, to the hierarchical reuse model. For this purpose, it is useful to define the special notation:

$$d = \frac{\tau_0}{T} \tag{6.12}$$

for the term that appears at the far right of (6.11). This ratio reflects how quickly data are written to disk relative to the overall lifetime of the data. We should expect its value to be of the same order as the ratio of "dirty" data items in cache, relative to the overall number of data items on disk. The value of d would typically range from nearly zero (almost no buffering of writes) up to a few tenths of a percent. Since a wide range of this ratio might reasonably occur, depending upon implementation, we shall adopt several contrasting values d as examples: $d = .0001$ (*fast destage*); $d = .001$ (*moderate destage*); and $d = .01$ (*slow destage*).

Also, in specializing (6.11), we may take advantage of (6.6), in that:

$$\tau_1 = f_1^{-1/\theta}\tau_0 = f_1^{-1/\theta}Td$$

Thus, in the case of the hierarchical reuse model, we obtain:

$$\frac{1}{u} = \frac{1}{u_h} + d(1 - \frac{u_1}{u_h})(f_1^{-1/\theta} - 1) \tag{6.13}$$

To define the best free space collection scheme, we must now specify the values of four variables: f_1, f_h, u_1, and u_h. These variables must satisfy (6.7), both as it applies to the pair of variables (f_1, u_1) and the pair of variables (f_h, u_h). They must also satisfy (6.13). Finally, they must produce the smallest possible number of moves per write, as given by (6.10). We are confronted, therefore, by a minimization problem involving four unknowns, three equations, and an objective function.

To explore the history dependent strategy, iterative numerical techniques were used to perform the minimization just described. This was done for a range of storage utilizations, and for the various values d just listed in a previous paragraph. The results of the iterative calculations are presented in the three dashed lines of Figure 6.1.

Figure 6.1 shows that fast destage times yield the smallest number of moves per write. Nevertheless, it should be noted that *prolonged* destage times offer an important advantage. Prolonged destaging provides the maximum opportunity for a given copy of the data, previously written by the host, to be replaced before that copy ever needs to be destaged. The ability to reduce write operations to disk makes moderate-to-slow destaging the method of choice, despite the increase in moves per write that comes with slower destaging.

If, for this reason, we restrict our attention to the case of moderate-to-slow destaging, the linear model provides a rough, somewhat conservative "ballpark" for the results presented in Figure 6.1. Putting this in another way, the linear model appears to represent a level of free space collection performance that should be achievable by a good history dependent algorithm. At low levels of storage utilization, however, we should not expect realistic levels of free space collection to fall to zero as called for by the linear model. Instead, a light, non-zero level of free space collection load should be expected even at low storage utilizations.

Chapter 7

TRANSIENT AND PERSISTENT DATA ACCESS

The preceding chapters have demonstrated the importance of incorporating transient behavior into models that describe the use of memory. By contrast, the models developed so far do *not* incorporate *persistent* behavior. Instead, for simplicity, we have assumed that interarrivals are independent and identically distributed. Since the assumed interarrival times are characterized by a divergent mean, this implies that, in the long run, the access to *every* data item must be transient.

The assumption of independent and identically distributed interarrivals is not vital, however, to most of the reasoning that has been presented. Of far more importance is the heavy-tailed distribution of interarrival times, which we have repeatedly verified against empirical data. Thus, the models presented in earlier chapters are not fundamentally in conflict with the possible presence of individual data items whose activity is persistent, so long as the aggregate statistical behavior of all data items, taken together, exhibits heavy-tailed characteristics. So far, we have not confronted the possibility of persistent access to selected data items, because the models presented in previous chapters did not require an investigation into statistical differences between one data item and the next.

In the present chapter, our objective is not so much to develop specific modeling techniques, but instead to build an empirical understanding of data reference. This understanding is needed in order to reconcile the modeling framework which we have pursued so far, with the practical observation that persistent patterns of access, to at least some data items, do happen, and are sometimes important to performance. We shall examine directly the persistence or transience of access to data items, one at a time. Two sources of empirical data are examined:

- I/O trace data collected over a period of 24 hours.

- Traces of file open and close requests, obtained using the OS/390 System Measurement Facility (SMF), collected over a period of 1 month.

The I/O trace data are used to explore reference patterns at the track image, cylinder image, and file levels of granularity. The SMF data allows only files to be examined, although this can be done over a much longer period.

It should be emphasized that the use of the term *persistent* in the present chapter is *not* intended to imply *any* form of "steady state". Over an extended period of time, such as hours or days, large swings of activity are the rule, rather than the exception, in operational storage environments. Such swings do not prevent an item of data from being considered *persistent*. Instead, the term *persistent* serves, in effect, to express the flip side of *transient*. Data that is persistent may exhibit varying (and unpredictable) levels of activity, but some level of activity continues to be observed.

Storage performance practitioners rely implicitly on the presence of persistent patterns of access at the file level of granularity. Storage performance tuning, implemented by moving files, makes sense only if such files continue to be important to performance over an extended period of time. The degree to which this condition is typically met in realistic computing environments is therefore a question of some importance.

Many formal studies have undertaken the systematic movement of files, based upon past measurements, so as to obtain future performance benefits. Some of the more ambitious of these studies, which have often aimed to reduce arm motion, are reported in [34, 35, 36, 37]. These studies have consistently reported success in improving measures such as arm motion and disk response time. Such success, in turn, implies some level of stability in the underlying patterns of use.

Nevertheless, the underlying stability implied by such findings has itself remained largely unexplored. Typically, it has been taken for granted. But the observed probabilities of extremely long interarrival times to individual items of data are too high to *allow* such an assumption to be taken for granted.

In this chapter, we shall find that data items tend to fall, in bimodal fashion, into two distinguishable categories: either transient or persistent. Those items which are persistent play a particularly important role at the file level of granularity, especially when the number of accesses being made to persistent files is taken into account.

The strong tendency of persistent files to predominate overall access to storage provides the needed underpinning for a performance tuning strategy based upon identifying and managing the busiest files, even if observations are taken during a limited period of time. If a file is very busy during such observations, then it is reasonable to proceed on the basis that the file is likely to be persistent as well.

As the flip side of the same coin, transient files also play an important role in practical storage administration. The aspects of storage management involving file migration and recall are largely a response to the presence of such data. The present chapter touches briefly on the design of file migration and recall strategies. The following chapter then returns to the same subject in greater detail.

1.   TRANSIENT ACCESS REVISITED

So far, we have relied on the statistical idea of an unbounded mean interarrival time to provide meaning to the term *transient*. It is possible, however, to identify a transient pattern of references, even when examining a single data item over a fixed period of time. For example, the process underlying the pattern of requests presented in Figure 1.1 appears clearly transient, based upon even a brief glance at the figure. The reason is that *no requests occur during a substantial part of the traced interval.*

To formalize this idea, consider the requests to a specific data item that are apparent based upon a fixed window of time (more specifically, the interval $(t, t + W]$, where t is an arbitrary start time and W is the duration of viewing). Let S be the time spanned by the observed activity; that is, S is the length of the period between the first and last requests that fall within the interval. The persistence P of a given data item, in the selected window, is then defined to be

$$P = \frac{S}{W} \qquad (7.1)$$

In the case of Figure 1.1, it would be reasonable to argue that the observed activity should be characterized as transient, because P is small compared with unity.

The hierarchical reuse model makes an interesting prediction about the behavior of the persistence metric P. This can be seen by picking up again on some of the ideas originally introduced in Subsection 4.2 of Chapter 1. It should be recalled, in the reasoning of Chapter 1, that the single-reference residency time τ may assume any desired value. Thus, we now choose to set $\tau = W$ (i.e. we imagine, as a thought experiment, the operation of a cache in which the single reference residency time is equal to the length of the time window).

Consider, now, the *front end* time, as previously defined in Chapter 1. By the definition of the quantity $\Delta\tau$, the rate at which such time passes, in units of seconds of front end time per second of clock time, is given by $rm\,\Delta\tau$. Also, by the reasoning previously presented in Subsection 4.2 of Chapter 1, the rate per second at which intervals are *touched* is given by:

$$rm(1 + \frac{\Delta \tau}{\tau})$$

where we assume that the time line is divided into regular intervals of length $\tau = W$. Therefore, the average amount of front end time per touched interval is:

$$\Delta \tau \left[1 + \frac{\Delta \tau}{\tau}\right]^{-1} = \Delta \tau (1 - \theta)$$
$$= W\theta$$

where we have made two applications of (1.11).

But, recalling that front end time begins with the first I/O and is bounded by the last I/O of a cache visit, that a single-reference cache visit has a null front end, and that no two I/O's from distinct cache visits can occur in the same interval, we have the following situation:

- Every touched interval contains all or part of exactly one front end.

- S can be no longer than the length of that front end or portion of a front end.

Based upon the average amount of front end time per touched interval, we may therefore conclude that

$$E[P] < \theta \qquad (7.2)$$

where strict inequality must apply due to cases in which the front end crosses an interval boundary.

In many previous parts of the book, we have used the guestimate $\theta \approx .25$. Keeping this guestimate in mind, (7.2) means that we should expect the examples of the hierarchical reuse model studied up until now to exhibit values of the persistence metric P that are small compared to unity.

It is important to note that the conclusion just stated applies *regardless of the interval length W*. To drive home the significance of this fact, it is useful to consider a thought experiment. As Figure 1.1 makes clear, patterns of I/O requests tend to be "bursty". Suppose, then, that we wish to estimate the number of requests in a typical I/O burst. One possible approach might be to insert boundaries between bursts whenever a gap between two successive I/O's exceeds some threshold duration. The average number of requests per burst could then be estimated as the number of requests per boundary that has been inserted. The results obtained from this approach might obviously be very sensitive to the actual value of the threshold, however.

An alternative approach, that avoids the need to define a threshold, would be to examine the activity apparent in time windows of various lengths. For window lengths much longer than the time needed to complete a typical burst, one might usually expect to see an entire burst, isolated somewhere in the window. But for window lengths shorter than this characteristic time, and assuming that such a characteristic time actually exists, one might usually expect to see some portion of a burst, spread throughout the window. The characteristic burst time, and the corresponding number of requests, could then be identified by the transition between these two patterns of behavior.

The result (7.2) is in sharp contrast, however, with the outcome of the thought experiment just presented. Patterns of reference that conform to the hierarchical reuse model, although bursty, do *not* preferentially exhibit bursts of any specific, quantifiable length. Instead, they are bursty *at all time scales*.

It is reasonable to hope, therefore, that individual transient or persistent data items can be distinguished from each other by applying the metric (7.1). Provided that the time window is long enough for the persistence of a given item of data to become apparent, this persistence should be reflected in a high outcome for P. On the other hand, regardless of the time scale, we may hope to recognize transient data from a small outcome for P.

Two I/O traces, each covering 24 hours at a moderate-to-large OS/390 installation, were used to investigate this idea. The two traced installations were:

A. A large data base installation running a mix of CICS, IMS, DB2, and batch.

B. A moderate-sized DB2 installation running primarily on-line and batch DB2 work, with on-line access occurring from a number of time zones in different parts of the world.

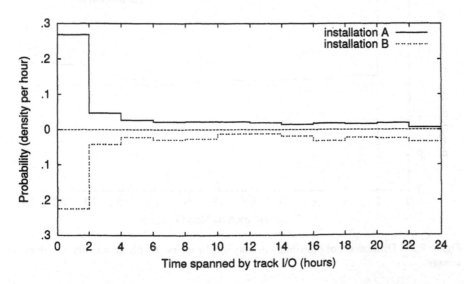

Figure 7.1.   Distribution of probability density for the metric P: track image granularity.

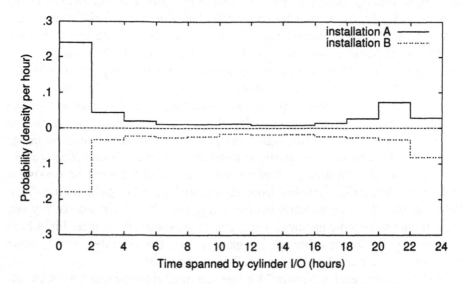

Figure 7.2. Distribution of probability density for the metric P: cylinder image granularity.

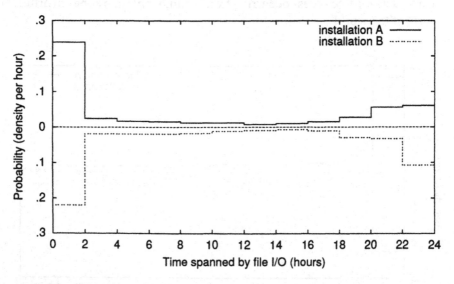

Figure 7.3. Distribution of probability density for the metric P: file granularity, weighted by storage.

Figures 7.1 through 7.3 present the observed distribution of the metric P for each installation. The three figures present distributions measured at three levels of granularity: track image, cylinder image, and the total storage containing a given file. Here files should be taken to represent the highest level of granularity, since the average file size tends to correspond to many cylinder images (9 in one recent survey).

The three figures show a pronounced bimodal behavior in the metric P. Individual data items tend strongly toward the two extremes of either $P \approx 0$ or $P \approx 1$. This appears to confirm the existence of the two contrasting modes of behavior, *persistent* and *transient*, as just proposed in the previous paragraphs. Based upon the region of P where the persistent mode of behavior becomes clearly apparent in the figures, we shall define the observations for a given data item as reflecting persistent behavior if

$$P \geq \frac{2}{3} \tag{7.3}$$

Otherwise, we shall take the observations to reflect transient behavior.

The figures also show that the role of persistent data is increasingly important at higher levels of granularity. Only a relatively few observed track images behave in a persistent manner; however, a substantial percentage of observed file storage was persistent, when measured at the file level of granularity.

2. PERIODS UP TO 24 HOURS

The analysis just presented was limited to studying the behavior of the metric P relative to a specific, selected time window of 24 hours. If we now use (7.3) to focus our attention specifically on the issue of whether observed behavior appears to be persistent or transient, however, it becomes possible to investigate a broad range of time periods. Such an investigation is important, since clearly any metric purporting to distinguish persistent from transient behavior should tend to show results that are robust with respect to the exact choice of time interval.

Figures 7.4 through 7.6 present the average percentage of storage capacity associated with track images, cylinder images, or files seen to be active at the two study installations, during windows of various durations, ranging from 15 minutes up to 24 hours. As we should expect, this percentage depends strongly on the granularity of the object being examined. Considered at a track level of granularity, it appears that only 10–20 percent of storage capacity tends to be active over a 24-hour period (based upon the two study installations); at a cylinder level of granularity, more like 20 to 40 percent of storage is active; and at a file level, 25 to 50 percent of the capacity is active.

Figures 7.7 through 7.9 explore *persistent* data at the same two installations. The three figures present the percentage of active track images, cylinder images,

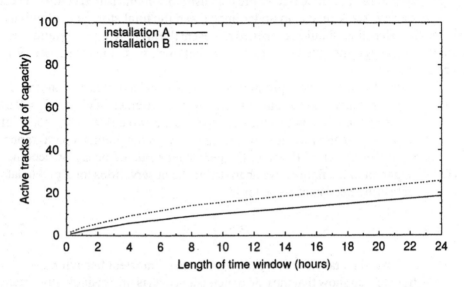

Figure 7.4.   Active track images as a function of window size.

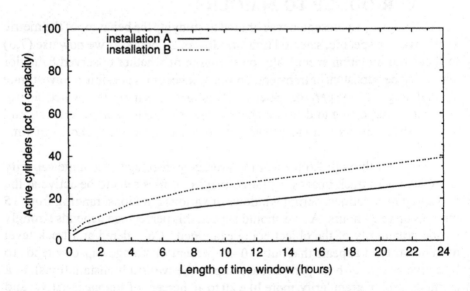

Figure 7.5.   Active cylinder images as a function of window size.

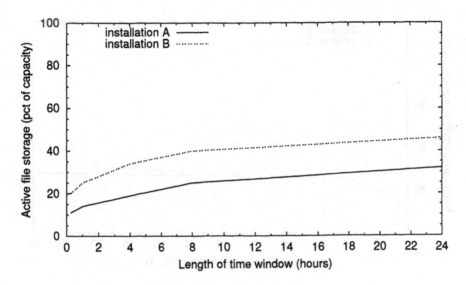

Figure 7.6.   Active file storage as a function of window size.

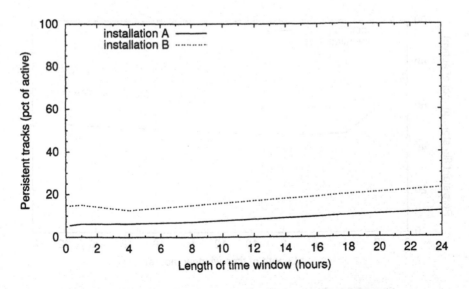

Figure 7.7.   Persistent track images as a function of window size.

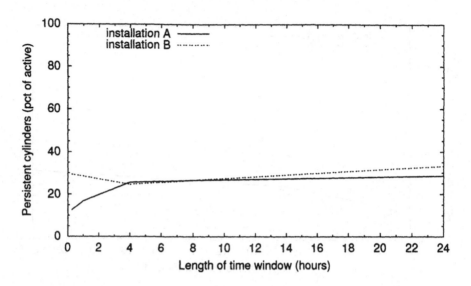

Figure 7.8.   Persistent cylinder images as a function of window size.

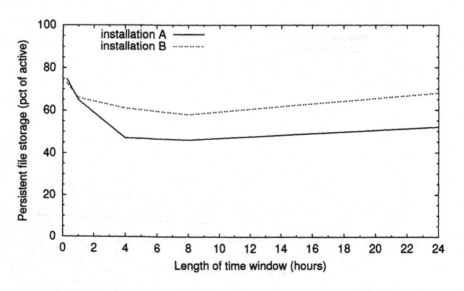

Figure 7.9.   Persistent file storage as a function of window size.

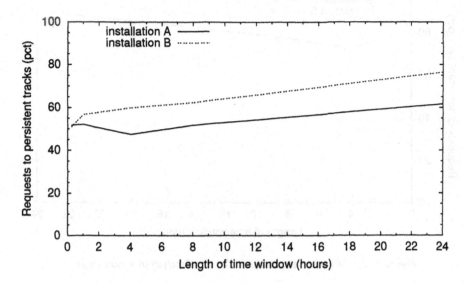

Figure 7.10.   Requests to persistent track images as a function of window size.

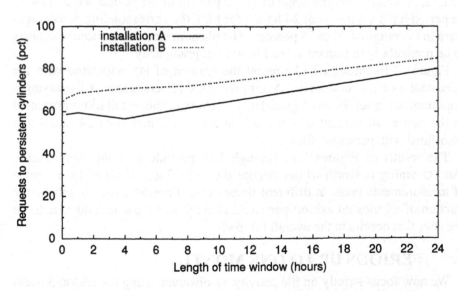

Figure 7.11.   Requests to persistent cylinder images as a function of window size.

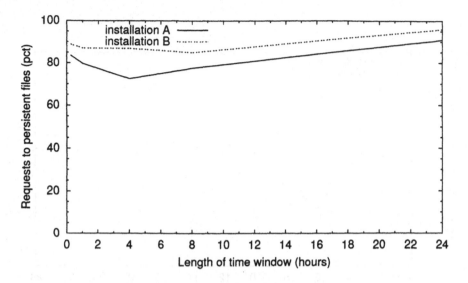

Figure 7.12.   Requests to persistent files as a function of window size.

and file storage that met the persistence criterion stated by (7.3). It should be noted that the percentage of persistent data depends even more strongly on the level of granularity, than does the percentage of active data. For track images, percentages in the range of 10-20 percent of active data were found to be persistent in a window of 24 hours; for files, the corresponding percentages were in the range of 50 to 75 percent. The phenomenon of persistence appears to be particularly important at the file level of granularity.

Figures 7.10 through 7.12 present the amount of I/O associated with the persistent data just discussed. Again, we see that persistence is increasingly important at higher levels of granularity. At both of the installations presented in the figure, 90 percent or more of the I/O over a period of 24 hours was associated with persistent files.

The results of Figures 7.10 through 7.12 provide a strong confirmation that I/O tuning is worth-while, despite the large fluctuations of load typical of measurements taken at different times or on different days. A substantial fraction of all files *do* exhibit persistent activity, and those that do tend to be the ones that dominate the overall I/O load.

3.   PERIODS UP TO ONE MONTH

We now focus strictly on file activity, as observed using the OS/390 System Measurement Facility (SMF). The use of SMF, rather than I/O tracing, allows much longer time windows to be analyzed. The results of this section are based mainly on the file open/close event traces contained in the SMF record types

14, 15, 62, and 64, plus miscellaneous other records relating to file creates, renames, and deletes. Due to the use of this source of data, I/O activity is accounted for based upon the software-supplied EXecute Channel Program (EXCP) counts, as placed into the SMF records just mentioned.

This section presents the results of a study in which SMF data over a period of one month was obtained at two OS/390 installations. These were:

C. A moderate-sized installation with a mix of on-line CICS, IMS, and DB2 database activity, plus TSO.

D. A large installation with on-line DB2 database, batch, and TSO activity.

Both installations had adopted active policies for Hierarchical Storage Management (HSM). At both installations, general-purpose (*primary*) disk storage contained, for the most part, only files referenced within the relatively recent past. The policies for the management of the remaining files, administered via System Managed Storage (SMS), called for SMS to *migrate* unused data, first to a compressed disk storage archive, then to tape after a further period of non-use. SMS would also *recall* such unused data, back to primary storage, on an as-needed basis.

To a remarkable degree, the files opened at both installations tended to be ones that had previously been open in the very recent past. Nevertheless, long gaps between open requests to a given file also occurred with a substantial probability. Figure 7.13 presents the resulting distribution of file interarrival times at each installation.

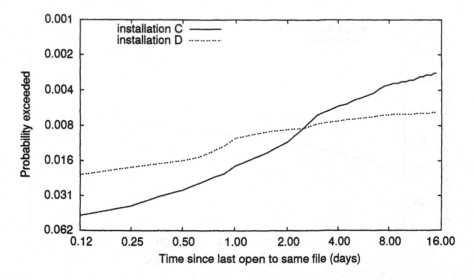

Figure 7.13.   Distribution of file interarrival times, based upon open requests.

It should not be surprising that the curves for both installations exhibit heavy-tailed behavior. Both curves appear to conform reasonably well to a mathematical model of the form (1.4), in that both resemble a straight line when plotted in a log-log format.

Very few requests (about .5 percent at installation C, for example) ask for data that have not been used for five days or longer. Thus, Figure 7.13 suggests that an HSM policy calling for migration of unused data after one week or more would have a good chance of being acceptable from the standpoint of application performance.

Figure 7.14 presents the average amount of storage associated with files that were active during various windows of time, ranging from about 15 hours up to 31 days. In cases where a file was created or scratched during a given study window, Figure 7.14 includes only the file's storage while allocated.

Figure 7.14 is adjusted, however, to ignore the impact of storage management. For example, if a file was migrated to tape during a given study window, then this action has no effect on the storage demand accounted for by the figure.

To understand the implications of Figure 7.14, it is useful to think through what the figure would look like in several specific examples:

1. A collection of static, continuously active files. In this case, the figure would be a straight, horizontal line.

2. A series of transient files which are created at random times, referenced at the time that they are created, not referenced afterward, and never scratched. The longer such files are allowed to accumulate (the more generous we are

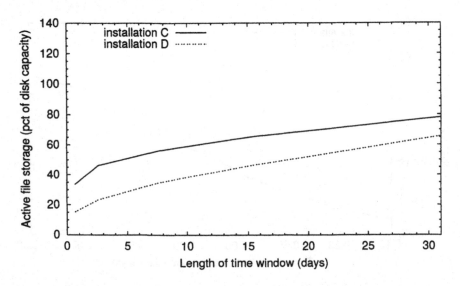

Figure 7.14.   Average active file storage over periods up to one month.

in defining which ones are "active"), the more storage they will require. Thus, this case would be represented by a straight line, sloping upward.

3. A series of transient files, which are created at random times, referenced at the time that they are created, not referenced afterward, and scratched after some waiting period. For files with this behavior, being created and scratched at a constant rate, the average amount of allocated storage s_{alloc} would not change with time. Since Figure 7.14 represents the average amount of allocated storage that is *active* within a specific window, the curves presented by the figure, for a case of this type, would always lie below s_{alloc}. Thus, at its right extreme, the curve would have a horizontal asymptote, equal to s_{alloc}. At its left extreme, for window sizes shorter than the shortest "waiting period", the curve would begin as a straight line sloping upward. Joining the two extremes, the curve would have a knee. The curve would bend most sharply at the region of window sizes just past the typical "waiting period".

The thought experiment just presented suggests that to discover transient data that are being created, but not scratched, we can look in Figure 7.14 for a *straight line, sloping up*. This appears to exist in the part of the curves past about 10-15 days, suggesting that most files that behave as in (3) will be scratched by the time they are one week old. Thus, a retention period of one week on primary storage again appears to be reasonable, this time relative to the goal of allowing data to be scratched before bothering to migrate it.

It should be emphasized that the cases (1-3) present a thought experiment, not a full description of a realistic environment. Any "real life" environment would include a much richer variety of cases than the simple set of three just considered.

Since the curves of Figure 7.14 deliberately ignore the impact of storage management, they help to clarify its importance. Without storage management, the demand for storage by transient files would continue to increase steadily. By copying such files to tape, their storage demand can be kept within the physical capacity of the disk subsystem. From the standpoint of the demand for disk storage, copying files with behavior (2) to tape makes them act like those of case (3) (except that the data can be, not just created, but also recalled). As long as the rate of creating and/or recalling transient files remains steady, the net demand for storage can be held to some fixed value.

Figures 7.15 and 7.16 present the role of *persistent* data as observed at the two study installations. The first of the two figures examines the fraction of active storage due to such data, while the second examines the resulting contribution to installation I/O.

Persistent files predominate I/O at the two installations, with 90 percent of the I/O typically going to such files (depending upon the installation and window

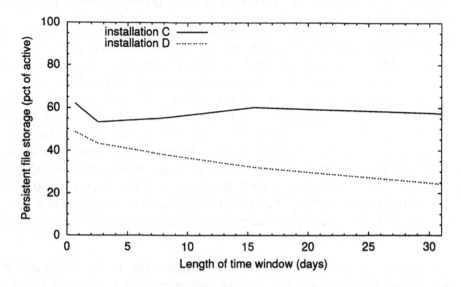

Figure 7.15.   Storage belonging to persistent files, over periods up to one month.

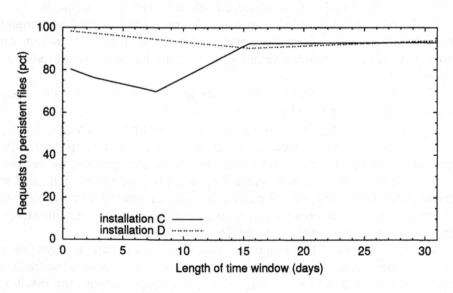

Figure 7.16.   Requests to persistent files, over periods up to one month.

size). Interestingly, the fraction of I/O associated with persistent files varies for window sizes of a few days up to two weeks; it then assumes a steady, high value at window sizes longer than two weeks. This suggests adopting a storage management policy that keeps data on primary storage for long enough so that files that are persistent within window sizes of two weeks would tend to stay on disk. Again, retention for one week on primary storage appears to be a reasonable strategy.

Our results for periods up to one month, as did the results for periods up to 24 hours, again seem to confirm the potential effectiveness of performance tuning via movement of files. Since the bulk of disk I/O is associated with persistent files, we should expect that the rearrangement of high activity files will tend to have a long-term impact on performance (an impact that lasts for at least the spans of time, up to one month, examined in our case study).

By the same token, the reverse should also be true: overall performance can be improved by targeting those data identified as "persistent". The properties of the persistence attribute (especially its stability and ease of classification into two bimodal categories) may make this approach attractive in some cases.

Chapter 8

HIERARCHICAL STORAGE MANAGEMENT

All storage administrators, whether they manage OS/390 installations or PC networks, face the problem of how to "get the most" out of the available disks — the most performance *and* the most storage. This chapter is about an endeavor that necessarily trades these two objectives off against one another: the deployment and control of hierarchical storage management. Such management can dramatically stretch the storage capability of disk hardware, due to the presence of transient files, but also carries with it the potential for I/O delays.

Hierarchical storage management (HSM) is very familiar to those administering OS/390 environments, where it is implemented as part of System Managed Storage (SMS). Its central purpose is to reduce the storage costs of data not currently in use. After data remain unused for a specified period of time on traditional (also called *primary* or *level 0*) disk storage, system software *migrates* the data either to compressed disk (*level 1*) or to tape (*level 2*) storage. Usually, such data are migrated first to level 1 storage, then to level 2 storage after an additional period of non-use.

Collectively, storage in levels 1 and 2 is referred to as *secondary* storage. Any request to data contained there triggers a *recall*, in which the requesting user or application must wait for the data to be copied back to primary storage. Recall delays are the main price that must be paid for the disk cost savings that HSM provides.

Hierarchical storage management has recently become available, not only for OS/390 environments, but for workstation and PC platforms as well. Software such as the Tivoli Storage Manager apply a client-server scheme to accomplish the needed migrations and recalls. Client data not currently in use are copied to compressed or tape storage elsewhere on the network, and are recalled on an as-needed basis. This method of managing workstation and PC storage has only begun to win acceptance, but offers the potential for the same dramatic storage cost reductions (*and* the same annoying recall delays) as those now achieved routinely on OS/390.

Many studies of hierarchical storage management have focused on the need to intelligently apply information about the affected data and its patterns of use [38, 39]. Olcott [38] has studied how to quantify recall delays [38], while Grinell has examined how to incorporate them as a cost term in performing a cost/benefit analysis [40].

In this chapter, we explore an alternative view of how to take recall delays into account when determining the HSM policies that should be adopted at a given installation. Rather than accounting for such delays as a form of "cost", an approach is proposed that begins by adopting a specific performance objective for the average recall delay per I/O. This also translates to an objective for the average response time per I/O, after taking recall activity into account. *Constrained optimization* is then used to select the lowest-cost management policy consistent with the stated performance objective.

Since the constrained optimization approach addresses recall delays *directly*, it is unnecessary to quantify their costs. The question of what a given amount of response time delay *costs*, in lost productivity, is a complex and hotly debated issue [41], so the ability to avoid it is genuinely helpful. In addition, the constrained optimization approach is simple and easily applied. It can be used either to get a back-of-the-envelope survey of policy trade-offs, or as part of an in-depth study.

The first section of the chapter presents a simple back-of-the-envelope model that can be used to explore the broad implications of storage cost, robotic tape access time, and other key variables. This section relies upon the hierarchical reuse framework of analysis, applied at the file level of granularity. The final section of the chapter then reports a more detailed study, in which simulation data were used to examine alternative hierarchical storage management policies at a specific installation.

1.   SIMPLE MODEL

This section uses constrained optimization, coupled with the hierarchical reuse framework of analysis, to establish the broad relationships among the key storage management variables. Our central purpose is to determine the amounts of level 0 and level 1 disk storage needed meet a specific set of performance and cost objectives.

Storage is evaluated from the user, rather than the hardware, point of view; i.e., the amount of storage required by a specific file is assumed to be the same regardless of where it is placed. The benefit of compression, as applied to level 1 storage, is reflected by a reduced cost per unit of storage assigned to level 1. For example, if a 2-to-1 compression ratio is accomplished in migrating from level 0 to level 1, and both levels use the same type of disk hardware, then the cost of level 1 storage would be one-half that of level 0.

Although we wish to determine the amount of primary disk storage by modeling, it is also desirable to ensure some minimum amount of primary storage. Even if the storage management policy specifies the fastest possible migration (migration after 0 days), some primary storage will still be needed for data currently in use, for free space, and as a buffer for data being migrated or recalled. The model allows this minimum storage to be specified as a fixed requirement.

Our storage management model therefore ends up using the following variables:

s_{00} = minimum primary storage (gigabytes).

s_0 = primary storage beyond the minimum (gigabytes).

s_1 = level 1 disk storage (gigabytes).

s_d = $s_0 + s_1$ = total disk storage beyond the minimum (gigabytes).

E_0 = cost of primary storage ($ per gigabyte per day).

E_1 = cost of level 1 storage, after accounting for compression ($ per gigabyte per day, $E_1 < E_0$).

D_0 = recall delay due to miss in level 0 = time to recall from level 1 (seconds).

D_1 = recall delay due to miss in level 1 = time to recall from level 2 (seconds, $D_1 > D_0$).

m_0 = level 0 miss probability per I/O (probability that the requested data is not at level 0).

m_1 = level 1 miss probability per I/O (probability that the requested data is neither at level 0 nor level 1).

D = target delay per I/O (seconds).

τ_0 = migration age (period of non-use) before migrating data from level 0 to level 1 (days).

τ_1 = migration age (period of non-use) before migrating data from level 1 to level 2 (days, $\tau_1 > \tau_0$).

In terms of these variables, we wish to accomplish the following

Constrained optimization version A: *Find the two values $s_d \geq s_0 \geq 0$, such that*

$$E_0 s_{00} + E_0 s_0 + E_1 s_1$$

is a minimum, subject to:

$$D_0(m_0 - m_1) + D_1 m_1 = D$$

Constrained optimization version A is not yet ready, however, to apply in practice. First, we must quantify how the level 0 and level 1 miss ratios m_0 and m_1 relate to the corresponding amounts of storage s_0 and s_d.

To keep terminology simple, let us focus on the recalls that must go beyond some specific level of the hierarchy in order to service an I/O request, while lumping together all of the storage that exists at this level or higher. Let m be the probability that a recall will be needed that goes outside of the identified collection of levels, which occupy a total amount of storage s beyond the minimum. Thus, m and s may correspond to m_0 and s_0, or may correspond to m_1 and s_d, depending upon the specific collection of levels that we wish to examine.

Now, some of the storage referred to by s will be occupied by data that has arrived there via recall and will leave via migration. Let this storage be called s_{cycle}, and let remaining storage (occupied primarily by files not yet migrated, and also by data that is in between being recalled and being scratched) be called s_{other}. Since the files in either component of storage can stay longer as the migration age increases, we should expect that both of these components of overall storage should increase or decrease with migration age. In hopes of getting a usable model, let us therefore try assuming that these two storage components are directly proportional to each other; or equivalently, $s_{cycle} = k_1 s$, for some constant k_1.

Since the data accounted for by s_{cycle} enters the corresponding area of storage via recall and leaves via migration, the behavior of this subset of storage is directly analogous to that of a storage control cache, in which tracks enter via staging and leave via demotion. It is therefore possible to apply the hierarchical reuse model, as previously developed in Chapter 1. By (1.23), this model predicts that

$$m = k_2 s_{cycle}^{-\theta/(1-\theta)} \tag{8.1}$$

for some constants k_2 and θ. If we now substitute for s_{cycle}, we are lead to the hypothesis that, for constants k and θ which depend upon the workload, the estimate

$$m = k s^{-\theta/(1-\theta)} \tag{8.2}$$

may provide a viable approximation for m.

It is important to emphasize that there is no reason to believe that s_{cycle} and s_{other} are *precisely* proportional; thus, the equation (8.2) obtained from this assumption is merely a mathematically tractable approximation that we hope may be "in the ballpark". The underlying hierarchical reuse model does offer one important advantage, however, in that it predicts significant probabilities of needing to recall even very old data. This behavior differs, for example, from that which would result from assuming an exponential distribution of times between requests [38]. The need to recall even years-old files is, unfortunately, all too common (for example, spreadsheets and word processors must retain the ability to read data from multiple earlier release levels).

It should also be recalled, by (1.4), that m is directly proportional to $\tau^{-\theta}$, where τ is the threshold age for migration. Thus, the calibration of θ at a specific installation can be performed if data are available that show the recall rates corresponding to at least two migration ages.

For example, at the installation of the case study reported in the following section, simulations were performed to obtain the recalls per I/O at a range of migration ages. These were plotted on a log/log plot, and fitted to a straight line. The estimate $\theta = 0.4$ was then obtained as the approximate absolute slope of the straight line.

At an installation where hierarchical storage management is in routine use, HSM recall statistics will include the recall rates corresponding to two specific migration ages (those actually in use for level 0 and level 1 migration). Based on these statistics, the value of θ can be estimated as:

$$\theta = \frac{ln(m_0) - ln(m_1)}{ln(\tau_1) - ln(\tau_0)}$$

Once a calibrated value of θ has been obtained, the value of k can be estimated as:

$$k = \left\{ k^{-(1-\theta)/\theta}(s_d - s_0)/(s_d - s_0) \right\}^{-\frac{\theta}{1-\theta}}$$

$$= \left\{ [m_1^{-(1-\theta)/\theta} - m_0^{-(1-\theta)/\theta}]/s_1 \right\}^{-\frac{\theta}{1-\theta}}$$

(other, more simple methods of calibrating k are also practical, but the formula just given has the advantage that it can be applied even without knowing s_{00}). At the installation of the case study, the estimate $k = .000025$ was obtained.

While on the subject of calibration, the parameter s_{00} should also be discussed. In the installation of the case study, this parameter was estimated as the primary storage requirement when simulating a migration age of 0 days (14.2 gigabytes). However, it is also possible to "back out" an estimate of this quantity from the statistics available at a running installation. For this purpose, let s_{prim} be the total primary disk storage (that is, $s_{prim} = s_{00} + s_0$). By again taking advantage of the recall rates corresponding to the existing migration policies, we can estimate that:

$$s_{00} = s_{prim} - \left(\frac{m_0}{k}\right)^{-\frac{1-\theta}{\theta}}$$

For the sake of modeling simplicity, it is also possible to assume $s_{00} = 0$. In this case, some amount of extra primary storage should be added back later, as a "fudge factor".

By taking advantage of (8.2) to substitute for m_0 and m_1, we can now put constrained optimization version A into a practical form. At the same time, we also drop the fixed term $E_0 s_{00}$ (since it does not affect the selection of the minimum cost point), and rearrange slightly. This yields

Constrained optimization version B: *Find the two values* $s_d \geq s_0 \geq 0$, *such that*

$$E_0 s_0 + E_1(s_d - s_0)$$

is a minimum, subject to:

$$D_0 k s_0^{-\theta/(1-\theta)} + (D_1 - D_0) k s_d^{-\theta/(1-\theta)} = D$$

This minimization problem is easily solved, using the method of Lagrange multipliers, to determine the best values of s_0 and s_d corresponding to a given set of costs and recall delays. The minimal cost occurs when:

$$\frac{s_0}{s_d} = \left(\frac{E_1}{E_0 - E_1} \frac{D_0}{D_1 - D_0} \right)^{1-\theta} \tag{8.3}$$

This is the most interesting result of the model, since it expresses, in a simple form, how the role of primary storage depends upon storage costs and access delays.

For completeness, the remaining unknowns of the model can now be obtained by plugging the ratio given by (8.3) into the original problem statement:

$$s_d = \left\{ \frac{k}{D} \left[D_1 - D_0 + D_0 \left(\frac{s_0}{s_d} \right)^{-\frac{\theta}{1-\theta}} \right] \right\}^{\frac{1-\theta}{\theta}}$$

$$s_0 = s_d \left(\frac{s_0}{s_d} \right) \tag{8.4}$$

$$s_1 = s_d - s_0$$

Returning to (8.3), this equation reflects an interesting symmetry between the impact of relative storage cost (E_0 versus E_1) and that of relative miss delay (D_0 versus D_1). In practice, however, the latter will tend to drive the behavior of the equation. For example, if we plug in values taken from the case study reported in the following section, (8.3) yields:

$$\frac{s_0}{s_d} = \left(\frac{E_1}{E_0 - E_1} \frac{D_0}{D_1 - D_0} \right)^{1-\theta}$$

$$= \left(\frac{23.5}{47 - 23.5} \frac{16.2}{90 - 16.2}\right)^{1-.4} \tag{8.5}$$
$$= (1 * .219)^{.6}$$
$$= 0.402$$

In this calculation, the compression of level 1 storage yields a two-to-one advantage in storage costs compared to level 0. This causes the factor $E_1/(E_0 - E_1)$ to equal unity. As this example illustrates, values not much different from $E_1/(E_0 - E_1) = 1$ are likely when level 1 and level 0 use the same type of disk device.

By contrast, the factor $D_0/(D_1 - D_0)$, which reflects the comparison of miss delays at level 0 relative to miss delays at level 1, will tend to be much less than unity. Typically, D_0 will reflect the time to copy and decompress data from disk (assumed above to be 16.2 seconds), while D_1 will reflect the time to complete a copy from some form of tape storage (assumed above to be 90 seconds, due to the planned use of robotics). A disparity in delay times of this order will lead to relatively light use of primary storage (in the case of the assumptions just stated, the value $s_0/s_d = 0.402$ as shown by (8.5)). This arrangement takes optimum advantage of compression to avoid tape delays. The greater the disparity in miss delays, the smaller will be the optimum percentage of level 0 disk storage. Conversely, if tape delays are reduced by tape robotics or other technology, then (8.3) indicates that there should be a corresponding increase in the use of primary storage.

Note that the result $s_0/s_d = 0.402$, as just calculated above, is a statement about *logical* storage. To obtain the corresponding statement about *physical* storage, we must examine the quantity

$$\frac{s_0}{s_0 + s_1/C} = \left[1 - \frac{1}{C} + \frac{1}{C}\left(\frac{s_0}{s_d}\right)^{-1}\right]^{-1} \tag{8.6}$$

where C is the level 1 compression ratio. Thus, given the assumptions just discussed in the previous paragraph, the *physical* ratio of primary to overall disk storage (neglecting the minimum primary requirement) should be $[1 - .5 + .5/.402]^{-1} = .573$.

To finish our example, we can apply (8.4), coupled with the objective $D = .136$ milliseconds, based upon matching current delays, to obtain:

$$s_{00} = 14.2$$
$$s_0 = 33.4$$
$$s_1 = 49.6$$

2.   A CASE STUDY

This section improves upon the analysis just presented, by taking into account a more complete picture of both costs and recall delays at a specific installation. The case study presented below was performed by capturing the SMF records related to storage management, so as to simulate alternative storage management policies against the captured data.

The installation of the case study was a moderate-sized OS/390 installation with a mix of on-line CICS, IMS, and DB2 data base activity, plus a small amount of TSO storage. Essentially all user and database storage was SMS-managed, and was contained in a management class called STANDARD. At the time of the study, policies in the STANDARD pool called for migration off of level 0 storage after 15 days, and migration off of level 1 storage after an additional 9 days. The SMF data used in the study covered a period of 33 days. One immediate purpose of reassessing the hierarchical storage management policies at this installation was to examine a planned installation of tape robotics.

The case study involved the following steps:

1. Capture the daily SMF 14, 15, 17, 64, 65, and other miscellaneous record types associated with storage management.

2. Extract the key SMF data, and accumulate at least 30 day's worth.

3. For each combination of level 0 and level 1 migration ages up to a level 1 migration age of 30 days, simulate the resulting migrations, recalls, storage requirements, and costs.

4. Input the simulation results into a software package capable of contour plotting.

5. Use graphical techniques (as described below) to perform a constrained optimization based on the costs and recall rates associated with each combination of level 0 and level 1 migration ages.

Steps 1-3 were performed using the SMS Optimizer software package [42]. The cost computation as performed in Step 3 included the storage costs just described in the previous section, as well as several additional costs such as the cost of tape mounts and the CPU cost to perform compression. The remaining steps were performed using the SAS software package [43], which tends to be widely available in OS/390 environments.

The constrained optimization of Step 5 was performed by taking advantage of the SAS *contour plot* capability. Figure 8.1 presents the contour plot that was used for this purpose.

More precisely, the figure shows an overlay of *two* contour plots: one exhibits lines of equal cost, the other exhibits a line of fixed performance. In either case, the key SAS statement needed looks like the following example:

```
PROC GCONTOUR DATA=SIMDATA GOUT=SAVGRAPH;
    PLOT L0AGE*L1AGE=RELCOST / LEVELS=0.93 0.95 0.97;
```

To produce Figure 8.1, this exact statement (plus embellishments for the axis labels, legend and other niceties) was used to obtain the three lines of the figure that correspond to management policies with a total simulated cost of 93, 95, or 97 percent of current costs. A second PROC GCONTOUR statement, similar to the example, was used to obtain the line that corresponds to management policies with an average recall delay per I/O equal to the current average delay. The two plots were then overlaid on top of each other.

Let us now examine Figure 8.1. As already discussed, the figure explores the entire range of level 0 and level 1 migration ages up to a level 1 migration age of 30 days. The current migration policy (15 days on level 0, plus 9 more days on level 1) is marked with a crosshair ("⊕"). The line going through this symbol shows all of the migration policies that have the same average delay due to recalls as that of the current policy.

Consider, now, the policies that lie along the line of current performance. This line crosses two others: those that reflect costs equal to 97 and 95 percent of the current costs. This means that by modifying the migration policies to match those at the two points of intersection, costs can be reduced by 3 or 5 percent respectively while maintaining the same average delay due to recalls.

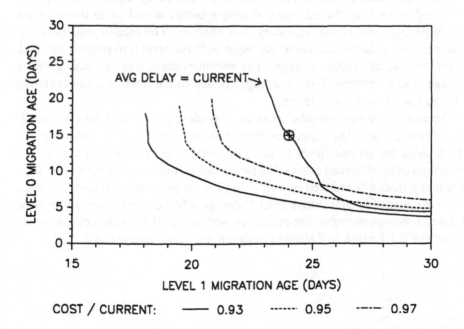

Figure 8.1.   Contour plot of the simulation results.

In addition, the fact that the line of current performance *crosses* the 95 percent line means that we can reduce costs still further. This can be done by following the current-delay line in the direction of lower costs. The minimum cost is achieved when the line of current performance just grazes a line of constant cost, without actually crossing it. As Figure 8.1 shows, this happens when the level 0 and level 1 migration ages are 5 and 27 days respectively, and when the cost is approximately 94 percent of its current value.

Again using the results of the simulation, the optimum storage management policies as just determined from Figure 8.1 can be translated back into storage requirements. In terms of the variables introduced in the previous section, the recommended amounts of storage are:

$$s_{00} = 14.2$$
$$s_0 = 30.6$$
$$s_1 = 70.8$$

These results refine and improve upon, while staying in essential agreement with, the corresponding back-of-the-envelope calculations presented in the previous section. Differences between the two sets of results are due to the much more complete handling of both costs and recall activity that is possible via simulation.

It is interesting to recall that, everything else being equal, the response indicated by (8.3) to the adoption of tape robotics would be to *increase* the use of primary relative to secondary disk storage. The recommendation just obtained above, however, was to *decrease* both the level 0 migration age and, hence, the use of primary storage. The recommendation to decrease primary storage, and to increase level 1 storage, is due to the starting point (existing policies) at the study installation.

The analysis just presented shows that, considering the long delays for recalls from level 2, the existing policies place too much emphasis on avoiding the much faster recalls from level 1. The introduction of tape robotics can reduce the length of level 2 recall delays; but nevertheless, our analysis shows that their frequency should be reduced as well. This is done by increasing level 1 storage at the expense of level 0. Since level 1 storage offers compression, an increase in level 1 storage improves the efficiency with which the existing performance objectives can be met, and allows a reduction in total storage costs.

Chapter 9

DISK APPLICATIONS: A STATISTICAL VIEW

As disk storage has evolved over the past several decades, a curious tension has developed between two key players in the capacity planning game. On one side of the dialog are those wishing to deploy a range of database applications that they see as being important to business growth or profitability. When examining plans for database deployment, the *storage cost*, as measured in dollars per unit of storage, appears to be the most important measure of any given disk technology.

On the other hand, those responsible for planning and managing the systems that must process transactions, running on the database, endeavor to point out the importance of disk performance. This side of the dialog often focuses on *access density* — the ratio of performance capability, in I/O's per second, relative to storage capacity in gigabytes. If some application requires a higher access density than a given disk technology can deliver, then for that application and type of disk, it is necessary to plan for less use of storage, and a higher effective cost, than those that appear "on paper".

The push and pull between the two key metrics just outlined — storage cost and access density — continues to recur as new generations of storage technology are introduced. Often, the debate focuses on the optimum storage capacity within a given family of physical disks. Those whose choice is driven by storage cost will consistently select the maximum feasible capacity; those whose choice is driven by access density will typically select the *smallest* available capacity.

This chapter tries to add to the dialog by providing a quantitative framework within which disk capacity, performance, and cost can *all* be considered. We also apply the proposed framework to answer two important questions:

1. Does a predictable relationship exist between storage cost and access density?

2. As advances in technology make possible disks with ever larger capacities and lower storage costs, what performance improvements are needed so that disk capacity, performance, and cost *all* remain in balance?

These questions are answered by introducing a simple but powerful model of storage applications. In this model, a wide range of potential applications are assumed to be possible, but only some of these are cost-effective to deploy at any given time. The performance requirements against a given storage technology thus become a function of the applications that are cost-effective on that technology.

In effect, the resulting *deployable applications* model of storage use extends the scope of our previous models to a level of the memory hierarchy deeper than the physical storage present at an installation at any given time. This hypothetical level contains those applications that *might*, in the near future, require storage, whether or not such applications have actually been implemented.

The parameters of the deployable applications model can be calibrated based upon historical trends. In this way, the model becomes a window on the recent history of disk storage, through which to better understand past events, as well as predict events in the future. Our answers to the two key questions framed above reflect what has occurred over the past several decades:

1. If storage costs fall, then application access densities, on average, should also be expected to fall, but at a slower rate. For example, a factor-of-two drop in storage costs should be expected to cause a drop in application access densities by approximately a factor of 1.6.

2. If disk capacity increases and disk storage cost decreases correspondingly, then disk performance should also improve to remain "in balance". For example, suppose that disk capacity increases by a factor of two, while storage cost falls by the same factor. Then we conclude that the performance of the new disk, as measured by its average service time per I/O, should improve by approximately 15 to 25 percent.

The deployable applications model may seem oversimplified to many readers. The model treats entire applications, which in a traditional capacity planning process must be tracked and forecast individually, on a statistical basis. Many capacity planners have found a need, however, to simplify the traditional process of capacity planning due to the increasingly large storage requirements involved and the relatively small amount of time and effort that can be budgeted for the planning process. The simplified, broad-brush nature of the deployable applications model may appeal to those practitioners who need a "back-of-the-envelope" alternative to traditional capacity planning.

The initial two sections of the chapter introduce the basic structure of the deployable applications model, and examine the calculation of application characteristics. The final two sections then turn to the implications of the model with respect to disk performance requirements, seeking a common ground between the two contrasting views outlined at the beginning of the chapter.

1. DEPLOYABLE APPLICATIONS MODEL

Consider an application a, with the following requirements:

v_a = transaction volume (transactions per second).

s_a = storage (gigabytes).

The purpose of the deployable applications model is to estimate whether such an application will be worthwhile to deploy at any given time. Thus, we must consider both the benefit of deploying the application, as well as its costs. Application a will be considered deployable, if its costs are no larger than its estimated benefits.

The *benefit* of application a is tied to desired events in the real world, such as queries being answered, purchases being approved, or orders being taken. Such real-world events typically correspond to database transactions. Therefore, we estimate the dollar benefit of application a from its transaction volume:

$$\text{benefit}_a = k_1 v_a \tag{9.1}$$

where k_1 is a constant.

For the sake of simplicity, we divide application *costs* into just two categories. Transaction processing costs, including CPU costs and hardware such as point-of-sale terminals or network bandwidth upgrades, are accounted for based upon transaction volume:

$$\text{processing cost}_a = k_2 v_a \tag{9.2}$$

where $k_2 \leq k_1$.

To account for the storage costs of application a, we examine the resources needed to meet both its storage and I/O requirements. Its storage requirements have already been stated as equal to s_a. In keeping with the transaction-based scheme of (9.1) and (9.2), we characterize application a's I/O requirement (in I/O's per second) as $G v_a$, where G is a constant (for simple transactions, G tends to be in the area of 10-20 I/O's per transaction).

Against the requirements of the application, as just stated, we must set the capabilities of a given disk technology. Let the disk characteristics be represented as follows:

p = price per physical disk, including packaging and controller functions (dollars).

c = disk capacity (gigabytes).

y = disk throughput capability (I/O's per second per disk).

$x = y/G$ = disk transaction-handling capability (transactions per second per disk).

D = average disk service time per I/O (seconds).

To avoid excessive subscripting, the specific disk technology is not identified in the notation of these variables; instead, we shall distinguish between alternative disk technologies using primes (for example, two alternative disks might have capacities c and c').

Based on its storage requirements, we must configure a minimum of s_a/c disks for application a; and based on its transaction-processing requirements, we must configure a minimum of v_a/x disks. Therefore,

$$\text{storage cost}_a = p \max\{\frac{s_a}{c}, \frac{v_a}{x}\} \qquad (9.3)$$

By comparing the benefit of application a with its storage and processing costs, we can now calculate its net value:

$$\Lambda_a = k v_a - p \max\{\frac{s_a}{c}, \frac{v_a}{x}\} \qquad (9.4)$$

where $k = k_1 - k_2 \geq 0$ represents the net dollar benefit per unit of transaction volume, after subtracting the costs of transaction processing.

For an application to be worth deploying, we must have $\Lambda_a \geq 0$. By (9.4), this requires both of the following two conditions to be met:

$$\frac{p}{x} \leq k \qquad (9.5)$$

and

$$\frac{s_a}{v_a} \leq \frac{ck}{p} \qquad (9.6)$$

Since the benefit per transaction k is assumed to be constant, our ability to meet the constraint (9.5) depends only upon the price/performance of the disk technology being examined. This means that, within the simple modeling framework which we have constructed, constraint (9.5) is *always* met, provided the disk technology being examined is worth considering at all. Thus, constraint (9.6) is the key to whether or not application a is deployable.

To discuss the implications of constraint (9.6), it is convenient to define the *storage intensity* of a given application as being the ratio of storage to transaction processing requirements:

$$q_a = \frac{s_a}{v_a}$$

The meaning of constraint (9.6) can then be stated as follows: to be worth deploying, an application must have a storage intensity no larger than a specific limiting value:

$$q_a \leq q_l = \frac{ck}{p} = \frac{k}{E} \tag{9.7}$$

where E is the cost of storage in dollars per gigabyte.

2. AVERAGE STORAGE INTENSITY

We have now defined the range of applications that are considered deployable. To complete our game plan, all that remains is to determine the *average* storage requirements of applications that fall within this range. For this purpose, we will continue to work with the *storage intensity* metric, as just introduced at the end of the previous section. Given that deployable applications must have a storage intensity no larger than q_l, we must estimate the *average* storage requirement $\bar{q}$ per unit of transaction volume.

Since it is expressed per unit of transaction volume, the quantity $\bar{q}$ is a *weighted* average; applications going into the average must be weighted based upon transactions. More formally,

$$
\begin{aligned}
\bar{q} &= \sum_a \left(\frac{v_a}{\sum_a v_a} q_a \right) \\
&= \frac{\sum_a s_a}{\sum_a v_a}
\end{aligned}
$$

where the sums are taken over the applications that satisfy (9.7). We shall assume, however, that the statistical behavior of storage intensity is not sensitive to the specific transaction volume being examined. In that case, $\bar{q}$ can also be treated as a simple expectation (more formally, $\bar{q} \approx E[q|q \leq q_l]$). This assumption seems justified by the fact that many, or most, applications can be scaled in such a manner that their storage and transaction requirements increase or decrease together, while the storage intensity remains approximately the same.

It is now useful to consider, as a thought experiment, those applications that have some selected transaction requirement — for example, one transaction per second. Storage for an application, within our thought experiment, is sufficient if it can retain all data needed to satisfy the assumed transaction rate.

There would appear to be an analogy between the chance of being able to satisfy the application requests, as just described, and the chance of being able to satisfy other well-defined types of requests that may occur within the memory hierarchy — for example, a request for a track in cache, or a request for a file in primary storage. In earlier chapters, we have found that a power law formulation, as stated by (1.23), was effective in describing the probability of being able to satisfy such requests. It does not seem so far-fetched to reason, by analogy, that a similar power law formulation may also apply to the probability of being able to satisfy the *overall* needs of applications that have some given, fixed transaction rate.

A power law formulation is also suggested by the fact that many database designs call for a network of entities and relationships that have an explicitly hierarchical structure. Such structures tend to be *self-similar*, in the sense that their organization at large scales mimics that at small scales. Under these circumstances, it is natural to reason that the distribution of database storage intensities that are larger than some given intensity q_0 can be expressed in terms of factors times q_0; that is, there is some probability, given a database with a storage intensity larger than q_0, that this intensity is also larger than twice q_0, some probability that it is also larger than three times q_0, and so forth, and these probabilities do not depend upon the actual value of q_0. If this is the case, then we may apply again the same result of Mandelbrot [12], originally applied to justify (1.3), to obtain the asymptotic relationship:

$$F(q) = 1 - \alpha q^{-\beta} \qquad (9.8)$$

where $\alpha, \beta > 0$ are constants that must be determined. In its functional form, this power law formulation agrees with that of (1.23), as just referenced in the previous paragraph. We therefore adopt (9.8) as our model for the cumulative distribution of storage intensity.

By applying (9.8), we can now estimate the needed average:

$$\bar{q} \approx E[q|q \le q_l] = \frac{1}{F(q_l)} \int_0^{q_l} q \, dF(q) \qquad (9.9)$$

As also occurred in the context of (1.11), the factor of q that appears in the integral leads us to adopt a strategy of formal evaluation throughout its entire range, including values q approaching zero (which, although problematic from the standpoint of an asymptotic model, are insignificant).

At first, the result of plugging (9.8) into (9.9) seems a bit discouraging:

$$\bar{q} \approx \frac{\alpha\beta}{1 - \beta} \frac{q_l^{1-\beta}}{1 - \alpha q_l^{-\beta}} \qquad (9.10)$$

This result is not as cumbersome as it may appear on the surface, however. Figure 9.1 shows why. When plotted on a log-log scale, the average storage intensity, as given by (9.10), is a virtually *linear* function of the maximum deployable storage intensity. The near-linear behavior stands up over wide ranges of the curve, as long as the maximum deployable intensity is reasonably large (indeed, each curve has a linear asymptote, with a slope equal to $1 - \beta$).

Consider a nearly linear local region taken from one of the curves presented by Figure 9.1. Since the slope is determined locally, it may differ, if only

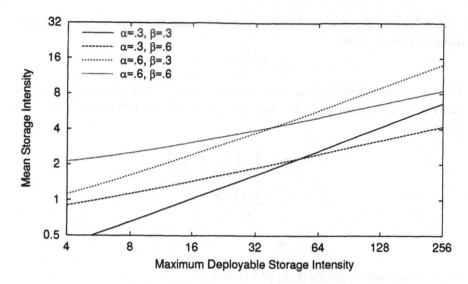

Figure 9.1.   Behavior of the average storage intensity function, for various α and β.

slightly, from the asymptotic slope of $1 - \beta$. Let the local slope be denoted by $1 - \hat{\beta}$. Suppose that the selected region of the chosen curve is the one describing disk technology of the recent past and near future. Then the figure makes clear that, in examining such technology, we may treat the relationship between average and maximum storage intensity as though it were, in fact, given by a straight line with the local slope just described; the error introduced by this approximation is negligible within the context of a capacity planning exercise. Moreover, based on the asymptotic behavior apparent in Figure 9.1, we have every reason to hope that the local slope should change little as we progress from one region of the curve to the next.

Let us, then, take advantage of the linear approximation outlined above in order to compare two disk technologies — for example, GOODDISK and GOODDISK', with capacities c and c', costs p and p', and so on. Then it is easy to show from the properties of the logarithm that

$$\frac{\bar{q}'}{\bar{q}} \approx \left(\frac{q_l'}{q_l}\right)^{1-\hat{\beta}}$$

But by (9.7), we know that

$$\frac{q_l'}{q_l} = \frac{E}{E'}$$

so

$$\frac{\bar{q}'}{\bar{q}} \approx \left(\frac{E}{E'}\right)^{1-\hat{\beta}} \tag{9.11}$$

In addition, the access density A and storage intensity q are, in effect, inverses of each other:

$$A_a = \frac{G v_a}{s_a} = \frac{G}{q_a}$$

This relationship applies, not just to individual applications, but also to aggregates of applications, since the average access density per unit of storage is given by:

$$\bar{A} = \sum_a \left(\frac{s_a}{\sum_a s_a} A_a \right)$$

$$= \frac{\sum_a G v_a}{\sum_a s_a}$$

$$= \frac{G}{\bar{q}}$$

We can therefore conclude from (9.11) that

$$\frac{\bar{A}'}{\bar{A}} \approx \left(\frac{E'}{E} \right)^{1-\hat{\beta}} \tag{9.12}$$

In words, this says that as the cost of disk storage falls, the access density of applications should also be expected to fall, but at a slower rate. Note, however, that the deployable applications model does not predict how much of a time lag should be expected between these events.

Equation (9.12) provides a convenient method of model calibration. As Figure 9.2 illustrates, both storage cost and access density declined steadily throughout the 1980's and early 1990's. From 1980 to 1993, storage costs fell at a compound annual rate of approximately 15 percent (from about 39 to about 5 dollars per megabyte), while access densities fell at a compound annual rate of approximately 11 percent (from about 9 to about 2.1 I/O's per second per gigabyte). Due to the reasonably steady nature of the process during this extended period of time, we can therefore conclude, even without knowing the specific time lag between cause and effect, that

$$0.89 \approx (0.85)^{1-\hat{\beta}}$$

or

$$\hat{\beta} \approx 1 - \frac{\ln(0.89)}{\ln(0.85)} \approx 1 - 11/15 \approx 0.3 \tag{9.13}$$

Here we have added slightly to the exact calculation so as to express $\hat{\beta}$ as a round number. The upward direction of round-off is the conservative direction; it corresponds, in the subsequent section, to adopting a slightly more demanding objective for disk performance than would have been the case if we had carried forward additional digits.

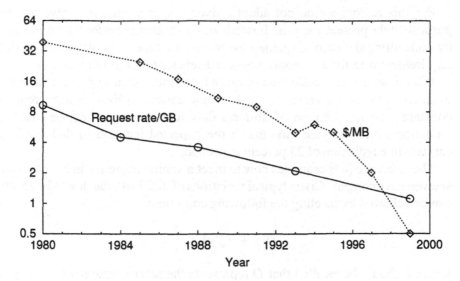

Figure 9.2.   Approximate trends in access density and storage cost.

3.   DISK PERFORMANCE REQUIREMENTS

The results just obtained apply directly to the assessment of disk performance for new generations of disks. For concreteness, consider the case in which, compared to GOODDISK, GOODDISK' has twice the capacity and half the cost per unit of storage. Then by (9.11), we should expect that, as a result of deploying GOODDISK', the average storage intensity of applications will increase by a factor of $2^{1-.3} = 1.62$. However, the amount of storage per disk increases by a factor of 2. Therefore, we must expect the net load per disk to increase by a factor of $2/1.62 = 1.23$.

In order for performance to stay "in balance" with the projected application requirements, the servicing of I/O requests must therefore speed up by enough to allow a 23 percent throughput increase.

Suppose, hypothetically, that we have adopted a fixed objective for the response time per I/O. Then an increase in throughput by some factor $1 + \delta$ (for example, the factor of 1.23 needed in the present analysis) can be achieved by reducing the service time per I/O by some corresponding factor $1 - \epsilon$, where we would expect that $\epsilon < \delta$.

While theoretically appealing, however, the reasoning just outlined does not "ring true". It is too risky to maintain a fixed response time objective while allowing service times to vary, since queue times may then also vary. The larger the queue time grows relative to service time, the more erratic the performance perceived by users of the system is likely to become.

For this reason, we do not adopt a fixed response time objective for the purpose of the present analysis. Instead, we aim to ensure performance *stability* by controlling the ratio of queue time to service time. The net result of this requirement is to force response times and service times to fall *together*.

If the load across a collection of disks is uniform, then to prevent the ratio of queue time versus service time from increasing, utilization must remain constant. So for the case of uniform disk load, we must require that the reduction in disk service time match the expected increase in disk load: a service time reduction of 23 percent is needed.

The reference [44] examines how to meet a similar objective in the case of a skewed environment. Given typical variations of disk load, the desired stability can be achieved by meeting the following condition:

$$D[y + 9\sqrt{y}] \leq \frac{2}{3}$$

where it should be recalled that D represents the service time per I/O and y is the average I/O rate per disk. To ensure that both GOODDISK and GOODDISK′ meet an objective of this form equally well, given that the load of the latter disk increases by a factor of $1 + \delta$ and its service time decreases by a factor of $1 - \epsilon$, we require that:

$$D(1 - \epsilon)[y(1 + \delta) + 9\sqrt{y(1 + \delta)}] \leq D[y + 9\sqrt{y}]$$

Since $\epsilon, \delta \ll 1$, we can simplify this condition using first-order Taylor expansions:

$$\delta \leq \epsilon \left(1 + \frac{4.5\sqrt{y}}{y + 4.5\sqrt{y}}\right) \tag{9.14}$$

Fortuitously, the factor that appears in prens on the right side of (9.14) is rather insensitive to the actual I/O load per disk y, provided that it is in a "reasonable" range. For example, if y is in the range $9 \leq y \leq 49$, then the factor on the right side of (9.14) is in the range $1.39 \leq$ factor ≤ 1.6. For "back-of-the-envelope" purposes, then, we can state the result of (9.14) as follows: in a skewed environment, the average throughput which a disk can sustain increases by a percentage roughly half again as large as the percentage by which the disk's service time per I/O can be reduced.

To achieve the throughput improvement of 23 percent that is needed for GOODDISK′, we therefore conclude that a reduction in service time in the range of 15 percent (for typical disk skews) to 23 percent (for no skew) will be required.

Since the results just stated might leave the impression that a skewed environment has some performance advantage compared with a uniform distribution of I/O across the disks supporting an application, it is important to emphasize that the reverse is actually the case. Any disk can deliver its best level of throughput per actuator in a uniform environment. The performance degradation due to skew is less, however, for a larger-capacity disk than for a smaller one. The required improvement in service time needed in deploying GOODDISK', as just stated above, takes into account this effect.

The needed reduction in service time can be (and historically, has been) accomplished in many ways. These include faster media data rate, shorter seek time, shorter latency, schemes to access the disk via multiple paths, higher path bandwidth, disk buffering and/or storage control cache, and many others.

What if GOODDISK' does *not* deliver the needed improvement in service time? For example, what if the I/O capabilities of GOODDISK' and GOODDISK are exactly the same?

The case of *no* improvement in performance is a useful extreme to examine. It helps to illustrate the difference between the conclusions of the deployable applications model, as just presented above, and those which would be reached by adopting performance objectives based upon access density.

Suppose that in some specific environment where GOODDISK is in use, storage capacity and performance are in perfect balance, so that GOODDISK's I/O capability and its capacity both run out at the same time. Also, suppose that the I/O capabilities of GOODDISK' and GOODDISK are the same. If we reason from performance objectives based upon access density, we must then conclude that the extra capacity offered by GOODDISK' has no value in the given environment, because it cannot be used. Therefore, we must consider that GOODDISK' has the same *effective* storage cost as GOODDISK, despite the fact that GOODDISK' offers twice the capacity at the same price.

Given these circumstances, the deployable applications model draws a different conclusion. It projects that the lower cost per unit of storage will enable a range of new applications, causing average access density to decrease, and average storage intensity to increase, by a factor of 1.62. Therefore, we can use up to 62 percent of the added capacity offered by GOODDISK'. As a result, GOODDISK' reduces the effective cost of storage by a factor of 1.62.

Given that GOODDISK' offers twice the storage of GOODDISK for the same price, the conclusion that *some* reduction of effective costs must occur as the result of deploying GOODDISK' seems compelling. As just shown, the deployable applications model provides a way to quantify the resulting effective cost, while also accounting for the performance of the new disk. Pulling the reasoning about GOODDISK and GOODDISK' into a systematic procedure, the steps of the method are:

1. Assume that disk capacity and performance are initially "in balance". More specifically, assume that the level of capacity use at which the old disk's I/O capability is exhausted (the *usable* capacity) is the same as its physical capacity.

2. Estimate the change y'/y in the I/O capability due to the new disk. For an environment with no skew of load across disks, the I/O capability should be expected to increase by the same ratio as the decrease in device service time. For an environment with skew, the change y'/y can be estimated based upon (9.14); or, as a "rule of thumb", the I/O capability can be increased by half again the percentage by which the service time falls. The factor y'/y represents an increase in usable capacity that comes with the new disk.

3. Use (9.11) to estimate the change $\bar{q}'/\bar{q}$ in storage intensity due to applications that the new disk enables. This factor also represents an increase in the usable capacity.

4. For performance to remain in balance with capacity, all of the new disk's physical capacity must continue to be usable:

$$\text{usable capacity}' = c\frac{y'}{y}\frac{\bar{q}'}{\bar{q}} \geq c' \tag{9.15}$$

or equivalently,

$$\frac{y'}{y}\frac{\bar{q}'}{\bar{q}} \geq \frac{c'}{c} \tag{9.16}$$

(with equality in the case where the disk remains in perfect balance).

5. If the new disk satisfies (9.16), its effective storage cost E'_{net} is the same as its nominal cost E'. If the new disk fails to satisfy (9.16), then its effective storage cost exceeds the nominal cost in proportion to the shortfall:

$$E'_{net} = E' \max\left\{1, \frac{c'/c}{(y'/y)(\bar{q}'/\bar{q})}\right\} \tag{9.17}$$

Equations (9.16) and (9.17) can be illustrated by validating our previous conclusions about GOODDISK'. We previously reasoned that an increase of 23 percent in I/O capability was needed for GOODDISK' to remain in balance, given an expected increase in storage intensity by a factor of 1.62. This agrees with (9.16), since $1.62 \times 1.23 = c'/c = 2$. If GOODDISK' delivers at least the required 23 percent improvement, then its effective cost will be the same as its nominal cost. We also reasoned that if GOODDISK' offers *no* improvement in performance, then its effective cost would be a factor of 1.62 lower than that of GOODDISK. This agrees with (9.17), since in this case the larger term within the maximization yields a right side equal to $E' \times 2/(1 \times 1.62) = (E/2) \times 2/1.62 = E/1.62$.

4.   CONCLUSION

As promised, we have applied the deployable applications model to demonstrate a cause-and-effect mechanism behind the historical linkage that has existed between storage cost and access density. The model is calibrated based upon, and reflects, the recent history of disk storage use. If storage costs fall, then access density should also be expected to fall, but at a slower rate. For example, a factor-of-two drop in storage costs should be expected to cause a drop in application access densities by approximately a factor of 1.6.

The concept of *usable capacity* is helpful in talking about the results of the deployable applications model. The usable capacity is the level of capacity use at which a disk's I/O capability is exhausted.

For a new disk to be "in balance", all of its physical capacity must be usable. In general, this will require improvements in disk performance to go along with any increases in disk capacity. If all of the capacity is *not* usable, then the effective storage cost will exceed the physical storage cost in proportion to the ratio of physical to usable capacity.

Our overall objective has been to reconcile two contrasting views, one emphasizing storage cost and the other access density. We have found, in the deployable applications model, some basis for *both* viewpoints:

1. Those concerned with the feasibility of applications are justified in focusing on storage cost, because, by (9.7), this is the primary driver that determines which applications are cost-effective to deploy.

2. Those concerned with system management are justified in emphasizing access density, because the effective cost of a given disk technology depends, in part, upon its ability to deliver the performance needed to make all of its capacity *usable*.

What the model adds is a way to link both views. The effective cost of a given disk technology depends, in part, upon its performance, and also, in part, upon the applications that it enables.

References

[1] J. Voldman, B.B. Madelbrot, L.W. Hoevel, J. Knight, P. Rosenfeld, "Fractal Nature of Software-Cache Interaction," IBM Journal of Research and Development, March 1983.

[2] D. Thiébaut, "From the Fractal Dimension of the Intermiss Gaps to the Cache-Miss Ratio," IBM Journal of Research and Development, November 1988.

[3] B. McNutt, "A Simple Statistical Model of Cache Reference Locality, and its Application to Cache Planning, Measurement, and Control," CMG Proceedings pp. 203-210, Dec. 1991.

[4] D.L. Peterson, R.H. Grossman, "Power Laws in Large Shop DASD I/O Activity", CMG Proceedings pp. 822-833, Dec. 1995.

[5] S.D. Gribble, G.S. Manku, D. Roselli, E.A. Brewer, T.J. Gibson, E.L. Miller, "Self-Similarity in File Systems," Proceedings of ACM SIGMETRICS, pp. 141-150, June 1998.

[6] M.E. Gómez and Vicente Sanonja, "Analysis of Self-Similarity in I/O Workload Using Structural Modeling," IEEE Int. Workshop on Mod. Anal. and Sim. Proceedings, pp. 234-242, 1999.

[7] C. Roadknight, I. Marshall, and D. Vearer, "File Popularity Characterization," Performance Evaluation Review, v. 27 no. 4, pp. 45-50, March 2000.

[8] E. Coffman, Jr. and P.J. Denning, *Operating Systems Theory*, Prentice-Hall, Inc., 1973

[9] E.J. O'Neil and P. E. O'Neil, "An Optimality Proof of the LRU-K Page Replacement Algorithm", Journal of the ACM, pp. 92-112, Vol. 46 No. 1, January 1999.

[10] M. Henley and I.Y. Liu, "Static versus Dynamic Management of Consistently Very Active Data Sets," CMG Proceedings, pp. 208-216, December 1987.

[11] C.P. Grossman, "Cache-DASD Storage Design for Improving System Performance," IBM Systems Journal, v. 24 nos. 3/4, pp. 316-334, 1985.

[12] B.B Mandelbrot, *The Fractal Geometry of Nature*, W.H. Freeman & Co., New York, revised edition, 1983. See particularly p. 383.

[13] B. McNutt, "An Overview and Comparison of VM DASD Workloads at Eleven Installations," CMG Proceedings pp. 306-318, Dec. 1989.

[14] J.D.C. Little, "A proof of the queueing formula: $L = \lambda W$," Operations Research v.9 n.3, pp. 383-387, 1961.

[15] C.K. Chow, "Determination of cache's capacity and its matching storage hierarchy," IEEE Transactions on Computers, pp. 157-164, Feb. 1976.

[16] A.J. Smith, "Cache memories," ACM Computer Surveys v. 14 no. 3, pp. 473-530, Sept. 1982.

[17] B. McNutt, "A Survey of MVS Cache Locality by Data Pool: the Multiple Workload Approach Revisited," CMG proceedings, Dec. 1994, pp. 635-643.

[18] B. McNutt, "High-Speed Buffering of DASD Data: A Comparison of Storage Control Cache, Expanded Storage, and Hybrid Configurations", CMG Proceedings, pp. 75-89, December 1990. See particularly appendix result (A-9), which becomes Equation (1.26) of the present book, when expressed in terms of miss ratios.

[19] N.A. Cherian and B. McNutt, "Method and Means for Generation of Realistic Access Patterns in Storage Subsystem Benchmarking and Other Tests," U.S. Patent no. 5,930,497, July 1999.

[20] N. Balakrishnan and A.C. Cohen, *Order Statistics and Inference: Estimation Methods*, Academic Press, 1991.

[21] D. Thiébaut, J.L. Wolf, and H.S. Stone, "Synthetic Traces for Trace-Driven Simulation of Cache Memories," IEEE Transactions on Computers, v. 41 no. 4, pp. 388-410, April 1992.

[22] B. McNutt and J.W. Murray, "A Multiple-Workload Approach to Cache Planning," CMG Proceedings pp. 9-15, December 1987.

[23] B. McNutt and B.J. Smith, "Method and Apparatus for Dynamic Cache Memory Allocation via Single-Reference Residency Times," U.S. Patent no. 5,606,688, February 1997.

[24] J.T. Robinson, M.V. Devarakonda, "Data Cache Management Using Frequency-Based Replacement," ACM SIGMETRICS Proceedings, pp. 134-142, v. 18 no. 1, May 1990.

[25] Y. Smaragdakis, S. Kaplan, and P. Wilson, "EELRU: Simple and Effective Adaptive Page Replacement," ACM SIGMETRICS Proceedings, pp. 122-133, v. 27 no. 1, June 1999.

[26] D. Lee, et. al., "On the Existance of a Spectrum of Policies that Subsumes the Least Recently Used (LRU) and Least Frequently Used (LFU) Policies," ACM SIGMETRICS Proceedings, pp. 134-143, v. 27 no. 1, June 1999.

[27] L.A. Belady, "A Study of Replacement Algorithms for a Virtual-Memory Computer," IBM Systems Journal, v. 5, pp. 78-100, 1966.

[28] J.K. Ousterhout and F. Douglis, "Beating the I/O Bottleneck: A Case for Log-Structured File Systems," ACM Operating System Review, pp. 11-28, v. 23, no. 1, January 1989.

[29] D.A. Patterson, G. Gibson, and R.H. Katz, "A Case for Redundant Arrays of Inexpensive Disks (RAID)," ACM SIGMOD Proceedings, pp. 109-116, June 1988.

[30] M. Rosenblum and J.K. Ousterhout, "The Design and Implementation of a Log-Structured File System," ACM Transactions on Computer Systems, pp. 26-52, v. 10, no. 1, 1992.

[31] J. Menon and L. Stockmeyer, "An Age-Threshold Algorithm for Garbage Collection in Log-Structured Arrays and File Systems," IBM Research Report RJ-101020, May 1998.

[32] B. McNutt, "MVS DASD Survey: Results and Trends," CMG Proceedings pp. 658-667, December 1995.

[33] P.J. Denning and J.P. Buzen, "The Operational Analysis of Queuing Network Models", ACM Computing surveys, v. 10 no. 3, pp. 225-262, September 1978.

[34] J. Wolfe, "The Placement Optimization Program: a Practical Solution to the Disk File Assignment Problem," ACM SIGMETRICS Proceedings, pp. 1-10, May 1989.

[35] P. Vongsathorn and S.D. Carlson, "A system fo adaptive disk rearrangement," Softw. Prac. Exp. v. 20 no. 3, pp. 225-242, March 1990.

[36] C. Ruemmler and J. Wilkes, "Disk Shuffling," HPL-91-156, Hewlett-Packard Laboratories, Palo Alto, CA, October 1991.

[37] S. Akyurek, "Adaptive Block Rearrangement," ACM Transactions on Computer Systems v. 13 no. 2, pp. 89-121, May 1995.

[38] R. Olcott, "Workload Characterization for Storage Modeling," CMG Proceedings pp. 705-716, Dec. 1991.

[39] M. Friedman, "Simple Models for Sizing Multi-level Storage Hierarchies," CMG Proceedings pp. 429-438, Dec. 1995.

[40] M.P. Grinell and M.J. Falendzsy, "A Financial Strategy for Configuration and Management of a DFSMSHSM Environment," CMG Proceedings pp. 220-239, Dec. 1995.

[41] A.J. Thadhani, "Interactive user productivity," IBM System Journal, Vol. 20, No. 4, pp. 407-423, 1981.

[42] *DFSMS Optimizer User's Guide and Reference*, IBM pub. order no. SC26-7047, February 1998.

[43] *SAS Language: Reference*, Version 6, First Edition, SAS Institute, Inc., Cary, NC (1990).

[44] B. McNutt, "DASD Configuration Planning: Three Simple Checks," CMG Proceedings, pp. 990-997, Dec. 1990.

Index

About the Author

Bruce McNutt is a senior scientist/engineer working in the Storage Subsystems Division of International Business Machines Corporation. He has specialized in disk storage performance since joining IBM in 1983. Among the many papers which he has presented to the annual conference of the Computer Measurement Group, as an active participant for more than fifteen years, are two that received CMG "best paper" awards. The present book brings to-gether two threads which have run through his work: the hierarchical reuse model of data reference, first introduced in 1991, and the multiple-workload approach to cache planning, first introduced in 1987. Mr. McNutt received his B.S. degree in mathematics from Stanford University, and his master's degree in electrical engineering and computer science from the University of California at Berkeley.